WAS THE INDUSTRIAL REVOLUTION NECESSARY?

Edited by
Graeme Donald Snooks

London and New York

940634

First published 1994
by Routledge
11 New Fetter Lane, London EC4P 4EE

Simultaneously published in the USA and Canada
by Routledge
29 West 35th Street, New York, NY 10001

Typeset in Garamond by
Ponting–Green Publishing Services,
Chesham, Buckinghamshire
Printed and bound in Great Britain by
Biddles Ltd, Guildford and Kings Lynn

British Library Cataloguing in Publication Data
A catalogue record for this book is available from
the British Library

Library of Congress Cataloging in Publication Data
Was the Industrial Revolution necessary? / edited by
Graeme Donald Snooks.
p.   cm.
Includes bibliographical references and index.
ISBN 0–415–10868–3
1. Industry–History.
I. Snooks, G.D. (Graeme Donald)
HD2321.W37   1994
338.09–dc20   93–45688
CIP

ISBN 0–415–10868–3
ISBN 0–415–10869–1 (pbk)

WAS THE INDUSTRIAL REVOLUTION NECESSARY?

The Industrial Revolution is one of the most enduring and studied areas of econmic history. However, recent studies have concentrated on reviewing existing literature rather than bringing a new perspective to bear on it.

Was the Industrial Revolution Necessary? takes an innovative look at this much discussed subject. The authors ask new questions, explore new issues and use new data in order to stimulate interest and elicit new responses. They look at it from various, previously unexplored angles. These include:

- The way the classical economists viewed natural resources as a constraint on rapid and sustained growth;
- How the Industrial Revolution might have appeared when looking forwards from the Middle Ages rather than the usual retrospective view;
- What contribution to the debate on living standards can be made by an understanding of income distribution within the family;
- What has been gained from these new explorations?

By examining the wider dimensions of the Industrial Revolution, the authors draw conclusions to answer the question of the title.

Graeme Donald Snooks is Coghlan Professor of Economic History at the Institute of Advanced Studies, Australian National University. He has published widely on a number of central issues in economic history and is editor of a number of prestigious book series and journals.

Also by Graeme Donald Snooks

DEPRESSION AND RECOVERY
Western Australia, 1929–1939

DOMESDAY ECONOMY
A new approach to Anglo-Norman history
(*With J. McDonald*)

PORTRAIT OF THE FAMILY WITHIN
THE TOTAL ECONOMY
A study in longrun dynamics:
Australia 1788–1990

HISTORICAL ANALYSIS IN ECONOMICS
(Editor)

ECONOMICS WITHOUT TIME
A science blind to the forces of historical change

Old stone to new building,
Old timber to new fires

T.S. Eliot

CONTENTS

FIGURES

TABLES

CONTRIBUTORS

Stanley L. Engerman   Professor of Economics and History, University of Rochester

R.V. Jackson   Fellow in Economic History, Research School of Social Sciences, Australian National University

Stephen Nicholas   Professor of Economic History, University of Melbourne

Deborah Oxley   Lecturer in Economic History, University of Melbourne

Graeme Donald Snooks   Coghlan Professor of Economic History, Research School of Social Sciences, Australian National University

E.A. Wrigley   Senior Research Fellow, All Souls, Oxford University

PREFACE

This book attempts to look at the Industrial Revolution in a number of new and interesting ways. It asks new questions, explores new issues, and uses new data in order to stimulate interest and to challenge new responses. It does not attempt to précis all that has been written in this field. There are a number of excellent books that do this very effectively. This book aims to encourage scholar, student, and layman alike to think anew about the Industrial Revolution. Economic history does not have to be dull. It *is* possible to be exacting but interesting. While some important new perspectives have been provided here, the main concern is that others will join in this new spirit and will help to create a much needed revolution in the study of the Industrial Revolution.

This book benefited from a one-day workshop at the Australian National University in July 1992 attended by a number of people with research interests in wider dimensions of the Industrial Revolution. We wanted to explore some possible new ways in this fundamentally important field. I was delighted that it attracted a wide audience of economic historians, economists, historians, and general lookers-on, and I hope that we can extend that audience through this book. It is pleasing that Alison Kirk and Alan Jarvis at Routledge believe we can.

The preparation of manuscripts for publication is always a hard and thankless job conducted under the tyranny of unreasonable deadlines set by editors and authors. It is a pleasure to be able to say, therefore, that my staff at ANU carried out this task in their usual expert and cheerful manner. In particular I wish to thank Jeannie Haxell and Ann Howarth for the wordprocessing, Barbara Trewin not only for the formatting but for keeping me to schedule, Wayne

Naughton for the programming and figure drawing, and Barry Howarth for the copy-editing and preparation of the index. Finally, I wish to thank Macmillan Press for granting permission to use material from Chapters 5 and 7 of my book *Economics without Time*.

G.D. Snooks
Sevenoaks
Canberra

1

NEW PERSPECTIVES ON THE INDUSTRIAL REVOLUTION

Graeme Donald Snooks

One of the oldest and most enduring fields of study in economic history is the Industrial Revolution. Since Arnold Toynbee first delivered his famous lectures on the subject at Oxford in the early 1880s, the Industrial Revolution has held an undiminished fascination for generations of economic historians, development economists, students, and the general public. The reason for this obsession is not hard to find – the Industrial Revolution is an event that marks the boundary between the modern period of economic growth driven by continuous technological change and earlier periods of human experience universally regarded as innocent of either rapid or sustained increases in real GDP per capita. It marked the first technological transformation – or 'technological paradigm shift' as I have called it elsewhere[1] – since the Neolithic Revolution about 10,600 years ago. Little wonder it has attracted so much attention.

But surely after a century of detailed investigation there is little more that needs to be said about this, albeit central, issue in the modern economic history of human society. Surely now the major priority – as in the latest scholarly book on the subject[2] – is to survey the vast existing literature on the Industrial Revolution so as to reach a consensus about this pivotal event. Once this has been done perhaps we should redirect our attention to economic change since the Second World War when revolutionary changes of another type – the shift of married female labour from the household to the market – occurred.[3] Certainly there is a need for much more work on this later period but, as I will show in this introduction, there are many more issues to be raised concerning the Industrial Revolution.

We have only begun to scratch the surface of a field that needs to be

1

ploughed long and deep. Even in areas which, at first sight, appear to be experiencing diminishing returns – such as the estimation of rates of growth and of changes in living standards – there is much fundamental work that remains to be done. We need to turn from reworking the estimates of others to constructing entirely new estimates based upon detailed new data sources as has been done recently with the new biological evidence. But even more importantly we need to view the Industrial Revolution from entirely different vantage points to those traditionally used. Indeed, the main objective of this book is to adopt a fresh approach to this well-worked field by asking new questions about: the wider role of the Industrial Revolution in human history; the contribution made by natural resources to this process; whether rapid and sustained growth is a modern invention; and what role the household played in the Industrial Revolution. New perspectives are required because many of the current interpretations can be traced back to the untested reasoning of the classical economists of the late eighteenth and early nineteenth centuries.

I 'OLD TIMBER TO NEW FIRES'

No attempt will be made here to provide a comprehensive account of the extensive literature on the Industrial Revolution; there are excellent surveys elsewhere.[4] Instead I will introduce the chapters that are to follow by indicating the extent and limitations of existing interpretations of the rate and nature of economic growth together with changes in living standards during the Industrial Revolution, and by suggesting how the new perspectives that are to follow provide helpful insights. Nor will an attempt be made in the introduction to critically evaluate the various chapters in this book, as that has been effectively done by Stan Engerman in Chapter 6.

GROWTH RATES

Early work on the Industrial Revolution by Arnold Toynbee (1884) and Paul Mantoux (1928) – and even T. S. Ashton (1948) – was more concerned with changes in economic structure and organization than with the rate of economic growth.[5] This contrasts with the present state of research which places much emphasis on the rate and timing of economic growth during the Industrial Revolution. When did this 'modern' preoccupation emerge? It is largely a product of the post-

Second World War concern of economists with Keynesian and neoclassical growth models, with the development problems of Third World countries, and with the modern growth accounting pioneered by Colin Clark, Simon Kuznets, and Richard Stone.[6] The foremost exponent of this new focus upon growth rates was Phyllis Deane (1965), who in turn was influenced by Simon Kuznets.[7] The slightly earlier work of W.W. Rostow on the ill-fated 'take-off', by contrast, was couched largely in the old-fashioned terms of structural change and was defined in terms of capital/output ratios rather than growth rates.[8]

In the mid-1960s, Deane made the enduring statement, which has been repeated by virtually every economic historian since then, that:

> Another characteristic of a pre-industrial community which distinguishes it from an industrialized one is that its level of living and of productivity is relatively stagnant. That is not to say that there is no economic change, no economic growth even, in a pre-industrial economy, but that such growth as does occur is either painfully slow or spasmodic, or is readily reversible. It is fair to say that before the second half of the eighteenth century people had no reason to *expect* growth.[9]

This vision of an abrupt increase in growth rates during the Industrial Revolution was interpreted by Deane as a product of structural change, largely due to the emergence of a rapidly growing industrial sector, and of technical innovation. More recently growth accountants, such as Nick Crafts and Knick Harley, have revised Deane's growth rate estimates downwards, as shown in Table 1.1, and have placed greater emphasis upon measuring the sources of growth.

Table 1.1 Old and new estimates of growth of national product per capita (compound rates)

Period	Deane and Cole %	Crafts %
1700–1760	0.45	0.31
1760–1780	-0.04	0.01
1780–1801	1.08	0.35
1801–1831	1.61	0.52

Note: The above growth rates would be only very slightly revised in the light of the recent (1992) revisions in Crafts and Harley, 'A restatement'
Source: Crafts, *British Economic Growth*, p. 45

Nevertheless they see the Industrial Revolution as a major discontinuity, with growth rates higher than in the pre-modern period.

In Chapter 4 of this book, Bob Jackson provides a skilful critique of the procedures employed both by Deane and Cole and by the revisionists Harley and Crafts. Jackson clearly shows just how indirect and precariously based these estimates really are before 1830. They are founded on just a few proxies – population, a sample of home industries, exports plus imports (or alternatively extra home industries), and net government expenditure. (This procedure makes the direct GDP estimates for 1086 presented in Chapter 3 look like the rock of Gibraltar.) Jackson argues persuasively that the differences between the initial Deane and Cole estimates and the revisions by Crafts and Harley largely 'reflect different assumptions about the workings of the economy rather than a deeper knowledge of what was happening during the Industrial Revolution', that 'the rate of economic growth during the Industrial Revolution remains an open question', and that a great deal of new detailed research is required to provide more objective estimates of growth rates.

Despite these revisions virtually all economic historians are still adamant that growth during the Industrial Revolution was much more rapid, and certainly more sustained, than whatever growth might have occurred in the pre-industrial period. They are prepared to make claims to this effect without discussing any quantitative evidence. The most recent (1993) position on this issue can be briefly summarized.[10] Joel Mokyr claims: 'The annual rate of change of practically any economic variable one chooses is far higher between 1760 and 1830, than in any period since the Black Death'. In the same volume David Landes writes: 'The rates of change [during the Industrial Revolution] were low by twentieth century standards, and also clearly lower than these historical income accountants had expected. But were they *low*? They were certainly not low by comparison with what had gone before . . . we also know that from the 1760s growth took an upward turn and proceeded at a higher rate'; and again, 'The Revolution was a revolution. If it was slower than some people would like, it was fast by comparison with the traditional pace of economic change.' Like others before, Landes substitutes for historical data the argument that: if we extrapolate growth rates of about 1.0 per cent or more backwards in time we quickly reach levels of income below subsistence. As shown in Chapter 3, this assumes, unhistorically, that growth is linear and that GDP per capita and consumption per capita are the same. Finally,

Knick Harley claims that real wages, the usual but invalid proxy for real GDP per capita, 'were without secular trend'.

Why, without consulting available quantitative evidence on real GDP per capita, are modern economic historians so convinced that rapid and sustained economic growth is a modern invention? It is difficult to say, but here are a few speculations. First, these scholars appear persuaded as to the relevance of the classical growth model, if not to the period of the Industrial Revolution when it emerged, at least to the pre-modern period. The classical model, on the assumption of diminishing returns with no technological change, predicts stagnation as the natural condition of economies. Although this prediction has not been quantitatively (or even qualitatively) tested for the period before 1700, many modern economic historians accept it as a matter of faith.

Secondly, there is general and uncritical acceptance of the flawed estimates of real 'wage' rates for the period 1264 to 1954 published by Phelps Brown and Hopkins in 1956.[11] This time series has been widely used as a proxy for real GDP per capita, despite the obvious problem (arising from a dramatically changing functional distribution of income) in doing so, and in the face of the many deficiencies of the underlying nominal 'wage' rate (actually piece rate) data, not least of which is its lack of representativeness (builders' workers in a rural economy). But consider what this index purports to show: that the level of real wages in 1477 was not exceeded until 1886! So much for the increase in labour productivity that is supposed to have occurred during and after – long after – the Industrial Revolution. The Phelps Brown index of real 'wage' rates is discussed in greater detail in Chapter 3, and the relevance of the classical growth model to pre-industrial society is dealt with by the author elsewhere.[12]

The final explanation as to why contemporary economic historians are willing to believe that stagnation was the lot of 'traditional' economies is that it is seen as an essential support for the notion of the Industrial Revolution *as a revolution*. But does this concept depend fundamentally upon the condition that any growth achieved during the Industrial Revolution, no matter how slow, must be more rapid and sustained than that in earlier periods? The short answer is no. The essence of the word 'revolution', according to the *Oxford Dictionary* is: 'complete change, turning upside down, great reversal of conditions (Industrial *Revolution*)'. What is essential, I wish to suggest, is not that society increased the overall pace of its activities, just that the 'complete change' or 'revolution' occur within a *relatively* short period of time, *when looking forward rather than backward.* The technological change involved in the Industrial Revolution took place over a period of about 70 years or about three generations. While this may not seem rapid when looking backward from the vantage point of the present, it does appear rapid when looking forward from the vantage point of the distant past. In particular, it was very rapid in comparison with the previous technological paradigm shift – the Neolithic Revolution – which took at least a millennium to unfold. And the Neolithic Revolution occurred far more rapidly than earlier forms of technological change. In examining the emergence of human society over very long periods of time we need to look forwards rather than backwards. The Industrial Revolution *was* a revolution, but not on the grounds of historically high rates of growth.

In Chapter 3, the author shows that rapid and sustained economic growth has been an inherent characteristic of Western Europe during the last millennium. Evidence is also provided to support the argument that, in contrast to the claim of Deane and others, economic decision-makers before 1760 did indeed have a reason to expect growth. They expected it because they invested in it. To claim that they did not expect it not only renders irrational the increase in the longrun capital/labour ratio, but also implies that pre-modern society was the product of exogenous, rather than endogenous, processes. Human society, according to this interpretation, is merely a straw in the wind.

THE GROWTH PROCESS

According to the conventional view, there was an abrupt change in the nature of the growth process before and after the Industrial Revolution. Once again it was Phyllis Deane who introduced this idea into the modern literature. In her influential book, *The First Industrial Revolution*, she claims:

> In effect, the levels of living in pre-industrial communities are not static in the sense of never changing, but are stagnant in the sense that the forces working for an improvement in output or productivity are no stronger over the long run than the forces working for a decline. An economy of this kind tends to be characterised by long secular swings in incomes per head, in which the significant variable is not so much the rate of growth

6

of output as the rate of growth of population. When population rose in pre-industrial England, product per head fell: and if, for some reason (a new technique of production or the discovery of a new resource, for example, or the opening up of a new market) output rose, population was not slow in following and eventually levelling out the original gain in incomes per head. Alternatively raised by prosperity and depressed by disease, population was ultimately contained within relatively narrow limits by static or slowly growing food supplies.[13]

Modern economic change, according to this view, is very different to pre-modern growth, which is alleged to be dominated by population change that always increases to extinguish any one-off increase in productivity. In contrast, after the Industrial Revolution population is unable to keep up with productivity change. This radical discontinuity is not explained. Why is it that Deane's 'new technique of production', which leads to an increase in productivity and output, does not give birth to further new technology? Why is it always overtaken by population? No answer is provided. And why, in the absence of annual quantitative data for real GDP per capita before 1688, was this view advanced? There appear to be two reasons. Usually there is an appeal to the work of Malthus (although there is a tendency to confuse his shortrun predictions with longrun historical outcomes) and to the real 'wage' rate index of Phelps Brown and Hopkins.

Although economic historians, even of the more economic kind, warn about viewing the real world through abstract models, they have ignored their own advice when using the classical model to explain the pre-modern world. Even the classical economists did not use their model in this way – they constructed it in order, unsuccessfully, to analyse the English economy towards the end of the Industrial Revolution. This is dealt with by Tony Wrigley in Chapter 2. But, it might be objected, we have evidence on real wage rates compiled by Phelps Brown and Hopkins. I have already called attention to some of the problems with this index. What must be emphasized here is that the Phelps Brown and Hopkins index actually fails to bear out the predictions of the classical model.

The classical growth model suggests that an increase in profits (from whatever cause) will lead to further investment, which in turn increases the demand for labour and causes money wages to rise, which encourages an increase in population, which requires the cultivation of additional but less productive land, which leads to an increase in production costs and a reduction of profits and wages, which causes investment and population to decline so that equilibrium or the stationary state is achieved. Real wages and population, therefore, are interactive – a change in one leads to a fairly quick response in the other and in the same direction. In other words, real wages and population follow each other in a lagged fashion (Malthus's 'oscillations') either upwards or downwards depending upon the stage of the longrun cycle, and only move inversely at turning points where population temporarily overshoots the economy's capacity to produce goods and services.[14]

The classical model, therefore, envisages a positive relationship between population and real wages in the longrun and an inverse relationship only in the shortrun. This is confirmed in Chapter 2 by Tony Wrigley who, examining the classical model in its own time, says: 'economic growth was normally accompanied by an increase in population'. But what does the Phelps Brown and Hopkins index show? It shows a longrun *inverse* relationship – of up to 200 years – between population and real 'wage' rates. This is not what the classical model predicts. Nor is it supported by the qualitative evidence of the pre-modern period. Also, it suggests that economic decision-makers in pre-industrial but 'developed' societies – as England was in the pre-modern period – were irrational. The available evidence enables us to reject such a view.[15]

Deane's view of the relationship between population and GDP per capita in pre-industrial societies is not unique. It is a particular favourite of historical demographers,[16] some medieval historians,[17] and has recently been endorsed by a quantitative economic historian. In the most recent (1993) book on the Industrial Revolution, for example, Knick Harley revives the forty-year-old Phelps Brown and Hopkins real 'wage' rate index – despite his criticism of it for the Industrial Revolution period as being too narrowly based[18] – and uncritically repeats the flawed conventional view that:

> In earlier centuries over long periods, real wages rose and fell in inverse relationship to population, but real wages were without secular trend . . . History conformed to economists' theoretical expectations, first developed by David Ricardo about 1800, that wages in an economy constrained by limited resources vary inversely with population.[19]

He notes in passing that, somehow, this inverse relationship became positive after Ricardo's time, but neglects to say why or how. Yet neither Ricardo nor Malthus, as suggested earlier, expected real wages and population to be inversely related in the longrun, only during shortrun 'oscillations'. In Chapter 3 it is shown that economic growth – as measured by real GDP per capita – proceeded via what I have called 'great waves of economic change' of about 300 years in duration, in which population, real GDP, real GDP per capita, and prices interact in a longrun positive, *not* an inverse, manner.

NATURAL RESOURCES AS A SOURCE OF GROWTH

Most surveys of the causes of the Industrial Revolution include a brief account of the relative supplies of natural resources.[20] While many authors regard the scarcity of natural resources as an incentive to provide substitutes through innovation, most of the detailed research in this area focuses upon the abundance of resources as a positive force – some would even say 'motor-force' – in the Industrial Revolution.[21]

In Chapter 2, Tony Wrigley investigates the role of natural resources and makes the important point that most discussions of the process of the Industrial Revolution focus upon supplies of capital and labour, and quickly pass over natural resources as if 'the changes needed to circumvent the restrictions of an organic economy were readily achieved and might be expected to occur naturally as part of a gathering momentum of growth'. Wrigley focuses, for purposes of illustration, on coal, the supply of which he regards as 'a necessary condition for the growth that took place': coal production was negligible in the mid-sixteenth century but, on the eve of the Industrial Revolution, exceeded 10 million tons per annum.[22]

Wrigley contrasts this relative neglect on the part of contemporary economic historians with the attitude of the classical economists whose 'pessimism [about future growth] stemmed from their views about . . . land, and each viewed its supply as posing problems, which there was no prospect of overcoming'. The value, he claims, in reviewing the writings of the classical economists lies in reminding us that, while we might take the supply of natural resources for granted, they saw it as *the* lion in the path of growth. He argues persuasively that greater attention should be given to the ways in which the limitations of the organic economy of England were overcome during the few centuries leading up to the Industrial Revolution. Had this been an easy matter, Wrigley suggests, 'the change would no doubt have occurred many centuries earlier'. But only, one might add, if the capacity to overcome natural resource constraints were a sufficient, as well as a necessary, condition for the Industrial Revolution to occur. This focus would appear to be relevant to the current debate over the future limits to growth.

URBANIZATION AND ECONOMIC GROWTH

A feature of the Industrial Revolution that has attracted considerable attention over the last century is the growth of the new industrial cities. Before the mid-eighteenth century, Britain had achieved only a limited degree of urbanization – about 15 per cent of its population.[23] Admittedly London had grown rapidly in the sixteenth and seventeenth centuries – from 70 to 600 thousand people[24] – but there was little urban growth elsewhere in the country. Not surprisingly, early observers, such as Mantoux and Nef,[25] in tracing the antecedents of the Industrial Revolution back into the past, looked for early signs of manufacturing and urbanization. Later generations of scholars, such as Landes,[26] have also associated economic growth with industrialization and urbanization, while Gunnar Persson has attempted to calculate longrun English growth rates using the changing degree of urbanization as a proxy.[27]

What these scholars have overlooked is that industrialization is not the only route to rapid and sustained economic growth. It should be well known that, in the nineteenth century, so-called 'regions of recent settlement' achieved relatively high rates of economic growth (and even higher rates of economic expansion) – in the case of Australia of 1.5 per cent per annum between 1860 and 1890 – by specializing in the exploitation of natural resources and exporting the resulting goods – mainly raw wool in the case of Australia – to Europe which had specialized in manufactured goods. In a similar way in the Middle Ages, England specialized in the exploitation of natural resources and the export of the resulting products – once again mainly raw wool – to those parts of Western Europe, namely the cities of Flanders and northern Italy, that had specialized in manufacturing, trade, and finance. Both rural England and urban Europe were able to grow rich in this interdependent way. The structure of the pre-modern economy does not necessarily indicate relative wealth or capacity to generate growth. But, as shown later in this chapter ('Sources of growth'), the non-urban character of Britain

10

in 1500 has been taken as evidence of its 'backward' and 'under-developed' character.

The origins of the British Industrial Revolution, therefore, should be sought not so much in earlier examples of manufacturing, but in the economic growth that was achieved by producing and exporting rural products. In this way Britain was able, over some seven centuries before 1760, to build up the infrastructure and institutional arrangements required to support the Industrial Revolution. The main precondition for the Industrial Revolution should be sought in the dynamic quality of England (and of Western Europe generally) throughout the pre-modern period, not in its economic structure. This is the subject of Chapter 3.

INCOME DISTRIBUTION BETWEEN AND WITHIN FAMILIES

If the Industrial Revolution is one of the most popular fields of study in economic history, then living standards must be one of the most hotly debated topics in this field. Ideology has made it so. Until about a generation ago, those claiming that the Industrial Revolution had depressed the living standards of the British working class were generally opposed to capitalism as an economic system (E.P. Thompson and E.J. Hobsbawm), whereas those claiming that living standards rose were generally supporters of capitalism (T.S. Ashton and R.M. Hartwell).[28] Over the past generation, however, the debate has been conducted less on ideological and more on empirical grounds. Even so, the variety of statistical evidence employed has not provided a clear-cut answer to the question: did British living standards rise or fall in the period 1760 to 1830?

Questions of living standards are always complex. There is no clear consensus about what it entails and it is rarely, if at all, examined within the context of the forces driving economic change. Often there is confusion between what economic decision-makers were actually attempting to do, and what historians think they should have been doing. We need to look at this issue anew. Basically the Industrial Revolution was an outcome of a highly competitive and aggressive struggle between economic decision-makers in various Western European kingdoms over a very long period of time. It was a struggle for material advantage that would confer on them the power to survive – what I have elsewhere called 'economic resilience' which can be effectively measured by real GDP per capita.[29] It is the pursuit of economic resilience rather than well-being that has driven European society. Before the Industrial Revolution economic growth led to the growing material standards of living of the ruling elite which, by the mid-eighteenth century, had been widened to include the middle classes. Given this fundamental objective of European society – an objective that generated growth in the pre-modern period as well as after 1760 – it would not be surprising if the living standards of the non-elite did not increase in the early stages of the Industrial Revolution. Improvement in the well-being of all was not uppermost in the minds of those who invested capital and introduced new technologies.

Another reason for the complexity of this issue is that material living standards can be thought of in a variety of ways: as GDP – or, more accurately, consumption – per capita; as the distribution of income between regions, families, and paid individuals; and as the distribution of 'income' within families. Most of the large existing literature has focused upon the first two at the expense of the third – distribution of income within families.

The most recent estimates of economic growth by Crafts and Harley suggest that real GDP per capita grew at a modest rate between 1760 and 1830. This positive growth is hardly surprising. The costs of achieving a technological paradigm shift had to have a positive pay-off as far as the economic decision-makers were concerned if it was to be carried through successfully over a period of two or three generations. While real GDP per capita is an appropriate measure of 'economic resilience' or the power to survive in an aggressively competitive environment, most argue, quite rightly, that it is not an appropriate measure of living standards. A better, but not perfect, measure is consumption per capita. The latest evidence on this indicator suggests that average consumption probably remained unchanged between 1760 and 1820 but then increased rapidly – somewhere between 45 per cent (Crafts) and 72 per cent (Feinstein) – between 1820 and 1850.[30]

The changing distribution of income (if not consumption) between the upper and growing middle-class families, on the one hand, and the working-class families, on the other, is reflected in the comparison between real GDP per capita and real wage rates. Work by Jeff Williamson suggests that real male wage rates for 'all' workers may have declined slightly (by 7 per cent) between 1797 and 1810, but thereafter increased rapidly – by a factor of 2.5 – to 1851.[31] There is, however, a hint in other research that paid female workers may have experienced declining real earnings in both rural and urban areas throughout the period.[32] If so, not only was there a shift in the gender distribution of income towards males, but total working-class income would have suffered more than male wage rates indicate. Finally, it should be realized that Williamson's suggestion of a distributional shift from workers to other income recipients before 1810 has not been accepted by scholars such as Feinstein, Crafts, Harley, and Jackson.[33]

Other data that might be expected to confirm or confound the wage and consumption data includes life expectancy, child mortality, and heights. The life expectancy data, unfortunately, only confuses the issue, suggesting a slight improvement before 1820 and little change between then and 1860.[34] Infant mortality in a relatively small number (seven) of parishes appears to have risen between 1813 and 1836, without any significant decline until *after* 1845.[35] Finally, the analysis of height data is no less obscure. In their pioneering study of British heights, Roderick Floud, *et al.* suggest that there *was* an increase in average heights, and hence of net nutrition, between 1760 and 1820, but that it *declined* between 1820 and about 1870.[36] More recently the work of Nicholas and Steckel (using independent convict data) and of Komlos (reworking the Floud, *et al.* data) suggests, possibly more convincingly, that there was a decline in average heights, and hence net nutrition, throughout the Industrial Revolution.[37] It is important to realize that heights are a function of net nutrition, not of average living standards, because of the non-consumption (of perishables) component of family income, which can move inversely with nutrition. Also it should be clear that while economic decision-makers attempt to maximize their material advantage they do not attempt to maximize heights.

The general picture after all this recent important work is much the same as it was a generation ago – working-class living standards did not change appreciably between 1760 and 1810, but thereafter they probably improved quite substantially. For the entire period 1780 to 1851, the consensus now appears to be that real wages and real GDP per capita probably increased, on average, by about the same amount – between 70 to 85 per cent.[38] Hence there was little redistribution over the entire period, but there would have been a degree of ebbing and flowing for shorter periods, particularly before the 1810s. And we should remember that there was considerable regional and sectoral variation, with the industrial north improving its position relative to the more prosperous rural south. But, of course, our view will change again the next time either the GDP or wage rate indexes are revised!

All this should be placed in its proper context: we would not necessarily expect an increase in working-class living standards between 1760 and 1820 as this was not the objective of those driving the early phases of the Industrial Revolution. Only after the 1820s did it become an essential condition for continuing the process of industrialization. The working class demanded, and were granted, a share of the action. This is why the pessimistic predictions of Marx failed to take place in Western capitalism.

A major gap in this large literature on living standards is the way in which income distribution *within* the family changed during the Industrial Revolution. An interesting attempt to fill this is made in Chapter 5 by Stephen Nicholas and Deborah Oxley. They argue that the Industrial Revolution led to a decline in the allocation of nutrients to girls within working-class households owing to the curtailment of women's employment opportunities in the market sector. As women in rural areas faced the least favourable employment opportunities, they experienced the greatest nutritional deprivation. The evidence for this argument comes from the height profiles of females in rural and urban areas in both England and Ireland derived from Australian convict data. In doing so they have utilized a rare source of data on females – a major omission in all living-standard research – and have opened up a new area of study.

WHY WAS BRITAIN FIRST?

While this question is not addressed directly in the following chapters, it can hardly be ignored here as it keeps recurring in the literature. The usual response is to provide a long shopping list of possible contributing factors. Mokyr's recent list is particularly intimidating, and mainly includes supply-side variables on the grounds that 'economists and historians alike have treated the common wisdom that necessity is the mother of invention with contempt'.[39] It includes natural resource abundance (or alternatively scarcity!); relative isolation; adequate supplies of skilled mechanics, and a practical empirical approach to solving technical problems; the 'right' kind of political and social structures, including property rights, patent laws, rational tax systems, laissez-faire attitudes, Poor Law provisions, and tolerance to deviant ideas; and the existence of extensive foreign trade (exporting 15 per cent of GDP in 1760); and so on. In other words,

Britain experienced the first Industrial Revolution because of the sum total of characteristics that went to make Britain unique in the mid-eighteenth century. This may be a fairly safe bet, but does it tell us more than the fact that Britain was Britain and the rest of Western Europe was not?

Surely the problem lies not so much with the answer but with the question which, in the main, reflects a misconception of the nature of the Industrial Revolution. The Industrial Revolution was not an exclusively British revolution as some have claimed,[40] but rather it was a Western European revolution. It was not possible for Britain to go it alone, in the way Western Europe had (largely) been able to. The Industrial Revolution emerged from a thousand years of fierce competition between a large number of small, equally matched Western European kingdoms. This struggle to take the lead in Europe had, over many centuries, been the spur to seek new ways of developing a larger surplus that could feed their military power. These new ways included a rate of technological change higher than that in classical antiquity,[41] together with an improvement in organizational form (the shift from feudalism to capitalism, largely involving the emergence of factor markets and the widening of commodity markets after the mid-eleventh century), and the expansion of trade. The role of intense military competition is also the reason for the success of Europe in contrast to China and other major civilizations. And it is why the 'Why Britain first?' question is irrelevant. Had it not been Britain it would have been another Western European country in the early nineteenth century. It was not a matter of Britain showing the way and the rest of Europe scrambling to catch up,[42] particularly as the growth experience of each country was different.[43] It was a tightly contested race, in which Britain passed over the line first but with the others in hot pursuit. In other words, the Industrial Revolution depended upon an interactive involvement of all Western European kingdoms in a longrun process of economic change.

II   THE HISTORICAL ROLE OF THE INDUSTRIAL REVOLUTION

As suggested in this survey, most economic historians regard modern economic growth as unique. While some of the following chapters cast doubts upon this view, they do not address the issue directly. Accordingly it will be dealt with briefly here. The basic question is: was the Industrial Revolution necessary for the emergence of the modern era? To answer this question we need to consider whether economic growth is a modern invention, whether the modern process of change is without precedent, and whether the modern distribution of income could have been achieved in any other way. These questions can be answered by placing the Industrial Revolution within the wider time frame of the past millennium.

IS GROWTH A MODERN INVENTION?

In Chapter 3 I have attempted to show that economic growth is not a modern invention. Growth – in terms of real GDP per capita – has been a fundamental characteristic of English society for at least the past millennium. The quantitative evidence presented in Chapter 3 shows that there was nothing unique about the Industrial Revolution in terms of rates of economic growth. Indeed, the English economy during the period 1086 to 1170 – a period of 84 years – grew at least as rapidly as it did during the height of the Industrial Revolution between 1801 and 1831 – a period of only 30 years. And during the first half of the sixteenth century growth rates were three times as great. Clearly rapid and sustained economic growth in England did not begin with the Industrial Revolution.

This new evidence suggests that growth has been an integral part of English society over the past 1000 years, and that it has proceeded in a cyclical manner (Figure 3.3, p. 65) through what I have called 'great waves' of economic change. In a competitive context these great waves are driven by a dynamic process that is both systematic and endogenous. The great waves, in other words, are not merely the result of random exogenous shocks as many social scientists have argued.[44] It would appear that in a highly competitive environment – and in the absence of severe external shocks – the internal dynamic in European society is capable of producing long upswings followed by periods of self-generated stagnation and downturn of approximately 300 years in duration. Also it is clear from the evidence presented in Chapter 3 that these great waves involve a positive relationship between population, real GDP, and prices on the one hand, and real GDP per capita on the other, rather than the inverse relationship claimed by many historians.

If, however, the external shocks are severe and prolonged, as they were during the onslaught of pestilence for the century or so after 1348, then the downturns will be more severe and prolonged, and the upswings will be shorter and more rapid, as they were during the first

16

half of the sixteenth century and again during the 1950s and 1960s. While these external events can constrain the outcome of continuous economic change, they are unable to extinguish it. In the absence of pestilence in the Middle Ages, it is highly likely that the second great wave would have been *about* 300 years in duration and the average rate of growth during the upswing would have been between 0.5 and 1.0 per cent per annum – similar to that in the eleventh and twelfth centuries and to that in the latter half of the Industrial Revolution. Similarly, in the absence of the distorting effect of the First World War on the 1920s, the shock of the Great Depression of the 1930s, and the dislocating impact of the Second World War on the 1940s, economic growth during the 1950s and 1960s – when the vicelike grip of external events was released – would not have been so rapid. The golden age would have been less golden and the interwar period would have been less lacklustre. None of this is meant to deny the existence of shorter cycles, as growth appears to proceed via cycles within cycles, with each responding to different levels of, and incentives for, investment.

It would help if we could place England's very longrun growth experience in a wider European and even Asian context. While GDP data are not available over the past 1000 years for continental Europe and Asia, it is possible to employ population data to sketch a wider context for England in terms of 'economic expansion' (of real GDP), if not of 'economic growth' (of real GDP per capita).[45] The interesting feature of Figure 1.1 is the close parallel between the three population series: each describes great waves of economic change of about 300 years in duration. Peaks were achieved between 1200 (China) and 1300 (Europe and England), about 1600, and again in the present; with troughs around 1400 and the 1650s. Owing to the highly competitive European environment, the close parallel between England and Europe suggests that the conditions, the responses, and the shocks were broadly similar throughout Western Europe during the past millennium. While China was also ravaged by plague (which began in China in 1331, spread to western Eurasia in 1346, and to Western Europe in 1348) in the fourteenth century – which would have led to a coincidence of the long downturn in population over these centuries – China's competitive environment differed markedly. After 1368 highly competitive external pressures faded away, as did innovation but not population increase.

Further, we can speculate that – given the positive relationship between population, real GDP, and real GDP per capita for England

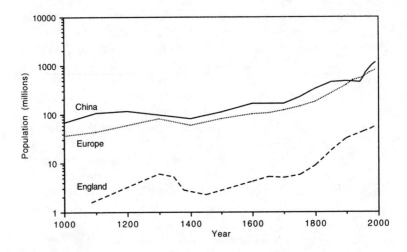

Figure 1.1 Population: China, Europe, and England, 1000–1990

Sources England: Snooks, *Economics Without Time*; Europe and China: McEvedy
and Jones, *World Populaiton History*; United Nations, *Demographic Yearbooks*
Note: Log scale on vertical axis

throughout the last 1000 years (Figure 3.3, p. 65) – fluctuations in real
GDP per capita similar to England's were experienced in Europe *as a
whole*. Owing to the very intense competition within Western
Europe between a relatively large number of small kingdoms, we
would anticipate a broadly similar growth pattern between the first
Industrial Revolution nation and Western Europe as a whole. If this
was not so, those kingdoms, or coalitions of kingdoms, that achieved
the most rapid economic growth, and hence political power, eventually would have absorbed those growing less rapidly. Despite a
millennium of military conflict between them, the map of Western
Europe looked much the same in the 1780s as it had done in the year
1000. No one kingdom had ever been able to dominate the whole of
the continent. True, the borders did move backwards and forwards,
particularly for Spain, Italy, France, and Germany, but the minor
triumphs of one kingdom were quite quickly overturned by another.
Political balance was maintained through economic balance. Certainly England grew no more rapidly than her sparring partners over
the very longrun, as her economic position in Europe in 1700 was
much the same as it had been in 1086.[46]

18

IS THE MODERN GROWTH PROCESS UNIQUE?

While the Industrial Revolution, therefore, was not necessary to achieve rapid and sustained economic growth either in England or Western Europe as a whole, could it have been necessary to achieve the type of growth that has occurred in the last two centuries? Is there, in other words, something unique about the nature, if not the rate, of modern economic growth? The short answer is yes. The Industrial Revolution involved what I have called a technological paradigm shift. During the late eighteenth and early nineteenth century there was, in other words, a fundamental change in the technological foundations of the British and, later, the European economies and their offshoots (USA, Canada, Australia). This caused a major change in the European economic system from one based upon agriculture to one based upon industry.

The earlier agricultural economy had begun with the Neolithic Revolution – the previous technological paradigm shift – in the Fertile Crescent some 10,600 years ago, had been developed in the pioneering civilization of Sumer, and had been handed down from one civilization to the next. Rome passed this economic system on to Western Europe which, over the following 1200 years, continued to fine-tune it to fit more effectively the very different conditions north of the Mediterranean.[47] The urban sector of post-neolithic society was highly dependent upon the agricultural sector, either directly or as a basis for trade, and was unable to achieve independent sustained growth. Trade between and within the kingdoms of Western Europe was both an expression of this growing prosperity and a contributor to it through the accumulation of wealth and the increasing capacity for specialization.

This technological fine-tuning of the agricultural and supporting sectors played a significant role in the economic growth of Western Europe during the millennium before the Industrial Revolution. Important also was the development of markets during this very long period. While English commodity markets contributed 40 per cent of GDP and foreign trade involved 20 to 24 per cent of GDP in 1086, factor markets – for labour, land, and capital – at that time were virtually non-existent. Over the following seven centuries, while the widening of commodity markets generated greater efficiency and, hence, growth, the main contribution was made by the emergence of factor markets. The emergence of factor markets between 1000 and 1200, as I have argued elsewhere, was central to the change in the

19

Western European economic system from feudalism to mercantile capitalism.[48]

In eleventh century England, land was distributed through the feudal system of subinfeudation by which the king granted land to his tenants-in-chief, and they in turn to subtenants, in return for promises of military support. Any land sales existed solely on the margins of this system. For similar reasons there was no labour market – the manorial system was a dependent form of agriculture in which labour was bound, under monopsony agreements between warlords, to the manor. Increases in the supply of labour, the scarce factor of production, could be obtained by the capture and sale of slaves (as capital not labour), but most commonly through natural increase or by additional grants of property complete with fixed capital and unfree peasants. Capital was also provided mainly through ploughed-back profits and property grants, together with finance from Jewish money lenders and, later, Italian and Flemish financiers and banks.

Between 1000 and 1300 in England rudimentary factor markets emerged and commodity markets were widened as new institutional arrangements became more efficient. The unfree peasants and slaves became either small tenants of manorial lords or landless labourers for hire on a piece-work basis. Local landmarkets developed, and capital markets emerged.[49] These developments reduced the costs of doing business (costs of transactions) – of obtaining land, labour, and capital, and of buying and selling commodities. The reduction in transactions costs,[50] together with steady technological change (the use of horses in ploughing, more efficient field rotation systems, improvements in water mills, the introduction of windmills, improved shipping, etc.),[51] greater specialization through trade,[52] and economies of scale, was responsible for the relatively rapid economic growth of this period. One could expect that those continued changes would have led to similar rates of growth in the period 1348 to 1490 had not Western Europe been held in the deathly grip of pestilence.

It has been customary to regard England at the end of the fifteenth century as an 'undeveloped country' and 'backward compared with most of the Continent'.[53] But this evaluation is not correct. In 1086 England was one of the wealthiest countries in Europe,[54] a position that had not been lost by 1160 towards the end of a period of rapid (0.6 per cent per annum) economic growth. While real GDP per capita in 1500 was only as high as that at the end of the previous boom owing to the effects of pestilence, this is not a good reflection of the technological and institutional changes that had taken place between 1350 and 1500. Also, this 'undeveloped country' had been able to put up a very credible performance against France during the Hundred Years War (1337–1453), throughout which England held south-west France and, briefly, after Agincourt (1415), the north of France, together with a promise of the French crown.[55] This sustained military advantage over France must have reflected a similar economic advantage. Also the rate of growth achieved between 1492 and 1560 suggests that considerable structural change had been occurring during the fifteenth century, which was masked by the effect of pestilence upon GDP per capita.

The usual comparison is between rural England and urban Flanders and northern Italy. In this respect, D.C. Coleman has said:

> England's one substantial commercial city, London, was over-shadowed in wealth and size as well as in political and cultural consequences by the great cities of continental Europe. It was about the same rank as Verona or Zurich; it did not compare with the greatest seaport in Europe, Venice; and nothing in England even began to match such a manifestation of wealth and power as the Medici family controlling the biggest financial organisation in Europe, with its base in Florence.[56]

But this misses the point. England grew rich in the tenth and eleventh centuries by specializing according to its comparative advantage – the growing and export of wool. In 1086 as much as 20 to 24 per cent of England's GDP was exported.[57] Cities in Flanders and northern Italy grew rich by importing raw materials such as wool, producing finished consumer goods, undertaking trade, and financing commercial activities. England was different to the city-states of Europe, but it was not significantly poorer – the very difference was the source of wealth on both sides of the English Channel. During the sixteenth century, with the declining export of wool and the growing export of textiles, and the rapid growth of London and other English city ports, this difference declined. Also it is not helpful to compare the wealth of a few cities, based upon the vagaries of international trade and finance, with the landed wealth of a kingdom that was to become the first industrial nation. As an acute observer of north Italian experience has said:

> We should not regard the rise of great families to new wealth, the lavish investment of wealth in new building and patronage,

or the spread of a new artistic sensibility and higher level of culture, as the sole characteristics of economic life in Renaissance Italy. Beside these indications of progress or prosperity we have to set the clear and constant evidence of peasant poverty and proletarian destitution.[58]

There may have been a difference in GDP per capita between the richest cities in Europe on the one hand and the rural aristocracy of England on the other – although this has yet to be demonstrated quantitatively – but England was certainly not an undeveloped country, or even relatively backward, in 1500.

Rapid growth in the sixteenth century was a response partly to the release of pestilence's grip, but mainly to rapidly expanding trade both within Europe and between Europe and the rest of the world.[59] This century saw the first breakout by the Europeans into the wider world. England, together with the Netherlands, was in a good position to exploit the commercial expansion of Europe and, indirectly through Spain, of the new world. For the 150 years before 1500, the English export of raw wool declined from 28,302 to 8,149 bags per annum, while woollen cloth increased from 3,024 to 13,891 equivalent bags.[60] But from 1500 to 1550 the number of 'shortcloths' increased 2.7-fold from 49 to 133 thousand[61] – a boom reflected in my estimates of real GDP per capita shown in Figure 3.3 (p. 65). The main buyer was Germany who, owing to a collapse of Italian production, could no longer purchase woollen cloth from its former suppliers. English products were particularly competitive in this period owing to the Tudor devaluation of the pound between 1522 and 1550. While woollen exports declined in importance after 1550 due to changing conditions of demand and supply on the Continent, other exports took their place including non-woollen textiles, iron, lead, military equipment, and glass. Iron production in England, for example, increased from 5,000 tons per annum in 1550 to 18,000 tons in 1600 and 24,000 tons in 1700; coal production increased from 0.21 to 1.5 million tons between 1550 and 1630, and had reached 11 million tons by 1800. British involvement in international trade also began to expand in the sixteenth and seventeenth centuries, with the total tonnage of merchant shipping rising from 50 to 340 thousand tons between 1572 and 1686.[62] This much could not have been achieved by a country that was still 'backward' in 1500.

Britain's involvement in international trade in the sixteenth and seventeenth centuries enabled greater specialization, which led to the type of economic growth that particularly impressed Adam Smith. By this time the changes in internal commodity and factor markets had slowed and would have been less important in the growth process of the sixteenth century than in that of the period 1000 to 1300. Changes in technology were still taking place, but their impact had declined.[63] Technological fine-tuning was definitely experiencing diminishing returns, as the limits of the late neolithic system were being progressively approached. Hence, the nature of the growth process in England differed significantly between the first and second great waves. What about the third?

The modern growth process – the third wave – ushered in by the Industrial Revolution, was entirely different to all that had gone before. For the first time technological change became the dominant force in economic growth. While this technological change eventually, and profoundly, transformed all sectors of the economy, it resided in the urban centres. For the first time in history, cities became centres of the sustained technological change that has driven Western civilization over the past two centuries. While the way we do business – the nature of the transactions between buyers and sellers of factors of production as well as goods and services – has also changed, it has been (and is) driven by technological change. As have been the changing patterns of international trade. Accordingly, the nature of economic growth during the third wave, which began with the Industrial Revolution, has been very different to that in both the first and second waves. Hence, it is the change in the nature of the growth process, rather than the rate of change of real GDP per capita produced by this process, that justifies the 'revolution' in the Industrial Revolution. It should be thought of as a technological paradigm shift.

The Industrial Revolution, therefore, was a necessary condition for the emergence of the modern era. But was it a sufficient condition? Were the changes that occurred during the traditional period of the Industrial Revolution – 1760 to 1830 – sufficient on their own to have caused this great technological paradigm shift? The short answer is no. The Industrial Revolution, like Rome, was not built in a day. And it was not built in an undeveloped country! Indeed, I wish to argue that, in the absence of the economic growth that occurred in the first and second waves, there would have been no third wave. The third wave depended upon three sets of conditions: the long slow build-up of economic infrastructure in England, and Europe as a whole, over a millennium or more; the prior development of non-organic sources of fuel and materials; and, as already discussed, the long, slow change in commodity and factor markets.

Without economic growth over the millennium before the eighteenth century, there would have been no build-up of capital stock in the urban and rural areas of Europe. The evidence for this capital accumulation in England and elsewhere is clear, particularly in the three centuries before 1300, and the century or so after 1490. It can be seen in the changing physical character of villages, towns, cities, and ports; it can be seen in the growing size and complexity of industrial establishments; and it can be seen in the growing sophistication of shipping.[64]

Over the seven centuries prior to the Industrial Revolution, two impressive great waves of economic growth made it possible for population to expand to a level (5.5 million in 1688), and to a standard of living, that pushed natural sources of organic fuels and materials to their limits. Before a new burst of sustained economic growth – the third wave – could occur, it was essential to develop new sources of energy and materials. Aspects of this issue are discussed in greater detail in Chapter 2 by Tony Wrigley.

Finally, the success of the Industrial Revolution depended upon the long slow transformation of the economic system – the shift from feudalism to mercantile capitalism. The essence of this transformation was the emergence of a system of flexible markets and market incentives that would make it possible to introduce a new process of technological change. This can only be seen in retrospect. It came about not because it was foreseen by longsighted decision-makers, but because self-interested individuals were seeking to maximize their material advantage.

WAS THERE ANOTHER ROUTE TO EQUALITY?

The other unique characteristic of modern economic growth is its democratization. Pre-modern growth, as we have seen, was impressive in terms of rates of change, but the growing surplus was monopolized by the ruling elite. In Domesday England a mere 0.5 per cent of the population held virtually all the country's wealth. Such an unequal distribution of income was necessary at that time in order to concentrate scarce resources in the hands of those who would invest rather than consume them. Over the period 1086 to 1700, the ruling elite was broadened – increasing from 0.5 per cent of the population to 16.5 per cent[65] – with the emerging middle classes. Nevertheless, only modern economic growth was capable of generating a reasonably equitable distribution of income – only modern growth has impacted upon the lives of the great mass of population in developed countries, as reflected in a large reduction in mortality and morbidity. The expected life at birth of males has increased from about 28 years in the eleventh century to about 33 years in the mid-fifteenth century, to 42 years by the late sixteenth century, 47 years by the late nineteenth century, over 60 years by the 1930s, and over 70 years by the 1990s.[66] Hence, while some improvement (about 18 per cent) can be noted before 1300 and again in the nineteenth century, the main increases in life expectancy at birth were experienced during the sixteenth century (by 27 per cent) and during the twentieth century (by 57 per cent). This closely reflects the three great waves of economic growth, and particularly the impact of the Industrial Revolution.

This is the outcome of a complex process involving an interaction between the changing size of real GDP per capita and the changing economic organization of society. In the eleventh century, when real GDP per capita was low relative to that at present, a surplus for investment could only be achieved if labour was paid much less than its marginal product. This was achieved through a feudal structure within which a monopsony agreement between the relatively small numbers of warlords prevented the free movement of scarce resources such as labour. With the growth of real GDP per capita, the breakdown of the feudal structure, the growth of labour markets, and the growing mobility of labour, relatively higher returns could and had to be paid to labour. This accelerated when workers received incomes sufficiently high to finance trade union activities, collective bargaining, and their own political parties. Needless to say, this has been a long slow process and has only changed dramatically since the mid-nineteenth century, and particularly since the mid-twentieth century.

Labour markets had emerged prior to the Industrial Revolution, but in rural areas they were still dominated by local squires, and in the towns and cities they were subject to restrictive laws.[67] Only with the sustained increase in the size of real GDP per capita and the accompanying changes in economic structure after the Industrial Revolution did labour gain the mobility and economic power to sweep those restrictions away. In this important sense the Industrial Revolution was necessary for a major redistribution of GDP and for a major improvement in the quality of life of all citizens in Western European society. Not just that of a few.

III CONCLUSIONS

The central claim in this book is that new light can be cast upon the Industrial Revolution by viewing it from previously unexplored vantage points. In the following chapters we look at the way the classical economists viewed natural resources as a constraint on rapid and sustained growth (Chapter 2); at how the Industrial Revolution appears when looking forwards from the Middle Ages rather than backwards from the present (Chapter 3); at what can be expected from growth rate calculations that have a substantially subjective basis (Chapter 4); at what contribution can be made to the living standard debate from an understanding of income distribution within the family (Chapter 5); and at what has been gained from these new explorations (Chapter 6). These are, of course, only a few of the possible new perspectives on the Industrial Revolution, and we hope that others may be encouraged to contribute to a major revolution in the study of the Industrial Revolution.

In exploring these new issues it has become clear that the Industrial Revolution was *not* necessary to achieve rapid and sustained economic growth. There were two earlier extended growth episodes in the pre-industrial European world. The Industrial Revolution, however, *was* necessary to maintain growth beyond the eighteenth century owing to the exhaustion of the late neolithic technological paradigm, and to achieve a more equitable distribution of income. Yet, while the Industrial Revolution was a necessary condition, it was not sufficient to achieve these outcomes. Without the economic growth generated during the millennium before the mid-eighteenth century, it would not have been possible to develop the infra-structure and organizational framework essential for the achievement of the Industrial Revolution and beyond.

2

THE CLASSICAL ECONOMISTS, THE STATIONARY STATE, AND THE INDUSTRIAL REVOLUTION

E.A. Wrigley

Since the human mind seeks understanding by looking for familiar patterns, it is no surprise that new elements on the scene are initially very hard to appreciate and are commonly assimilated to some existing scheme. In this sense it is not perhaps remarkable that the classical economists should have displayed so little awareness of the revolutionary economic changes which, it is now conventional to suppose, were taking place in England during their lifetimes. Adam Smith, David Ricardo, and Robert Malthus between them spanned the decades from about 1770 to about 1830, the 'classic' period of the first industrial revolution, but their writing is free from any discussion of such revolutionary change and of any sign that they had an inkling of its imminence. But, more than this, each of the three greatest of the classical economists found good reason to deny that change of this sort was possible. Each envisaged growth, though both possible and desirable (and evident in the past two centuries of English history), as necessarily limited and tending towards a future 'stationary state'.

The purpose of this chapter is to consider whether we can learn something about the nature of the Industrial Revolution from their attitudes and arguments. In particular their writings may serve to bring into focus an aspect of the Industrial Revolution which is sometimes neglected, for it connoted changes which for the first time allowed societies to escape from the constraints that are necessarily attendant upon all organically based economies. In such economies the problem of expanding raw material supply, and especially the related problems associated with the very modest energy supply maxima that prevailed, must curb growth with increasing severity as expansion takes place. The principle of the inevitability of declining marginal returns to land, one of the three basic factors of all material production in the analytic framework employed by the classical economists, has close parallels with the type of constraints imposed by an organic economy, though the two concepts are not identical. In this sense the Industrial Revolution represents the vanquishing of the growth curb which occasioned Ricardo's pessimism. Overcoming the limitations of an organic economy was a necessary condition for the occurrence of an industrial revolution. It was not, of course, a sufficient condition, but it is helpful to place the change in the forefront of the description and analysis of economic development in England in the quarter millennium after 1600, since it provides a convenient context for the discussion of other aspects of change. It is also an effective starting point for the consideration of the distinctiveness of English experience in the early modern period.

Adam Smith's worries about future growth stemmed in part from what he believed to be true of recent European economic history and in part from general considerations. While he had no means of measuring rates of return on investment, he argued that the prevailing rate of interest must be an acceptable proxy for this,[1] and noted that in Holland, the most economically advanced of all European states, the rate of interest was lower than anywhere else, and that it was next lowest in England which was the next most advanced. The rate in Holland was very low indeed. The government was able to borrow at 2 per cent and 'private people of good credit at 3 per cent'.[2] He attributed the pattern of interest rates to the differing scale of remaining opportunities for profitable investment in the different countries and argued that the progressive tendency for the rate of return on capital to fall signified the steady exhaustion of the finite stock of opportunities for investment that would yield an attractive return. Since employment opportunities were very closely linked to the outlay of capital, as growth slowed down real wages would fall:[3]

> In a country which has acquired that full complement of riches which the nature of its soil and climate, and its situation with respect to other countries, allowed it to acquire; which could, therefore, advance no further, and which was not going backwards, both the wages of labour and the profits of stock would probably be very low.[4]

This was the stationary state. Over a preceding period, which might be continued for a substantial time, the return to capital and labour might be much more favourable, but growth brought with it its own inevitable nemesis.

Ricardo developed an analogous argument that led him to a similar conclusion, founded on the concept of declining marginal returns on the land. At a slightly earlier date Malthus had formulated a closely similar proposition.[5] If all, or almost all, forms of material production require the combination of three basic factors of production, land, labour, and capital, and if one of the three, land, is in fixed supply, it must be the case that at some point as agricultural output expands larger and larger inputs of capital and labour will be needed in order to secure a unit increase in output both at the intensive and extensive margins of production. Ricardo recognized, of course, that improvements in agricultural technology might postpone the evil day, but thought that it was idle to hope for more than a temporary reprieve. His conclusion was unequivocal:

> Whilst the land yields abundantly, wages may temporarily rise, and the producers may consume more than their accustomed proportion; but the stimulus which will thus be given to population, will speedily reduce the labourers to their usual consumption. But when poor lands are taken into cultivation, or when more capital and labour are expended on the old land, with a less return of produce, the effect must be permanent. A greater proportion of that part of the produce which remains to be divided, after paying rent, between the owners of stock and the labourers, will be apportioned to the latter. Each man may, and probably will, have less absolute quantity; but as more labourers are employed in proportion to the whole produce retained by the farmer, the value of a greater proportion of the whole produce will be absorbed by wages, and consequently the value of a smaller proportion will be devoted to profits. This will necessarily be rendered permanent by the laws of nature, which have limited the productive powers of the land.[6]

To the arguments of Smith and Ricardo, Malthus had added other considerations which suggested a gloomy future. His depiction of the necessary tensions between production and reproduction, initially formulated as the contrast between arithmetic and geometric rates of increase, though very substantially modified in later life, suggested additional reasons to suppose that the condition of the labouring poor was unlikely to improve.[7] If the bulk of the population must make do on an income level which covers only the necessities of life, this too must set severe limits to the extent and nature of economic growth through its effect on the structure of demand.

With the benefit of hindsight the fears of the classical economists appear unjustified. Rates of return on capital investment have not fallen lower and lower. Declining marginal returns on the land have proved a chimera, and indeed the land, at least in the sense understood by the classical economists, no longer appears as an inevitable element in all material production. It has proved possible to induce exponential rates of growth in the economy at a level higher than population growth and, in any case, population in the developed countries has long lost any tendency to rise exponentially or, indeed, to maintain a positive link with economic growth.[8] Economic growth has brought with it other fears, to the point where it is now questionable whether indefinite growth is compatible with a safe and stable environment. But no-one fears a future which bears a close resemblance to the stationary state of the classical economists.

The fears entertained by the classical economists were not, however, quick to disappear. In the middle decades of the nineteenth century John Stuart Mill wrestled rather inconclusively with the issue of long-term growth, aware both of the intrinsic merit of the arguments advanced by his predecessors and of the scale of the extraordinary growth in industrial output of which there was abundant evidence. He appears to have thought the optimistic and pessimistic arguments closely balanced and was uncertain enough about the future of the living standards of the labouring poor to have pressed the case for birth control partly on this account.[9]

Contemporaries of the classical economists and they themselves were, of course, perfectly well aware of the technological developments of the age. Newcomen engines; many miles of turnpike roads; a rash of new canals; spinning jennies and mules; textile factories; new docks, harbours, and lighthouses; mining pumps; coke-fired furnaces, all attracted attention among informed men and women. New production sites and the new manufacturing towns were frequently visited by those who wished to be abreast of new developments or were moved by mere curiosity. Englishmen were well aware that their economy was exceptionally successful and were not bashful in asserting its strength, even though occasionally visited by doubts about its durability, especially in time of war. Although the extent of their acquaintance with such matters may be difficult to establish in detail, it is impossible to doubt that Adam Smith, Robert Malthus, and David Ricardo were as knowledgeable in these matters as most of their contemporaries.

Such knowledge, however, did not shake their pessimism about the medium-distance future. To us this may seem paradoxical; to them it did not, and in reflecting on this contrast perhaps an aspect of the transition which is too easily overlooked comes into clearer focus.

Pre-industrial economies were dominated by negative feedback. The process of growth itself made further growth progressively harder to secure. It is ironic that the reason for this should first have been formulated with clarity just when the analysis was about to become obsolescent. The division of the basic factors of production into three elements and the examination of their interrelationship was a leading feature of the writings of the classical economists and their insight into the role of one of these three, the land, was fundamental to their pessimism and to their conclusions about the stationary state. Given their assumptions, their conclusions appeared very well grounded. To appreciate their viewpoint it is important to recognize that almost all raw materials of value to man were either vegetable or animal in origin. Every major industry of the pre-industrial period either used such raw materials exclusively or was substantially dependent upon them. The vast majority of those in secondary employment used wool, cotton, flax, hemp, straw, leather, hair, fur, bone, meat, cereals, or wood as their raw materials. Even the metal industries, for example, together with the manufacture of ceramics and glass, required a source of heat for smelting or baking, which in turn meant access to an abundant supply of wood.[10]

Furthermore, farming and forestry, upon which all else depended, were closed entities ecologically and in relation to energy in pre-industrial circumstances. It was impossible to transform agricultural productivity by the deployment of large quantities of fertilizer produced off the farm, and it would have been suicidal to have created a situation in which the input of energy into farming was larger than the energy output from farming (a very common situation in industrialized countries today). A ceiling to output from the individual farm was set by the scale of photosynthesis by plants useful to man and cultivated by him. There was a wide range of practices which could raise the level of output commonly found in early modern England and bring it closer to the notional ceiling. English farmers had been unusually successful in the seventeenth and eighteenth centuries in narrowing the difference between the theoretical maximum and that actually reached and, still more remarkably, had succeeded in doubling output per man in the process;[11] but the general restriction remained. Although Ricardo may not have had precisely this consideration in mind when he wrote of 'the laws of nature, which have limited the productive powers of the land', he probably had in mind this same general obstacle to unlimited expansion.

The underlying problem was simple. Economic growth connoted higher levels of output. Higher levels of output meant inducing more production from an area of cultivable land that could not be significantly increased, and although the location of the output ceiling might be difficult to establish, it was clear that, as it was approached more and more nearly, further advance must become progressively more difficult. Since economic growth was normally accompanied by an increase in population, the difficulty was compounded by the problem of meeting the rising demand for the necessities of life occasioned by the increase in numbers. Hence the near certainty that the approach towards the stationary state would be accompanied by declining real wages and by a tendency for the return to capital also to decline.

The pessimism of the classical economists was to prove unjustified. The changes which were already in train in their day have proved more momentous in some respects than any that preceded them. Above all the Industrial Revolution made poverty problematic for the first time in human history. It had always previously seemed idle to suppose that the mass of the population could hope to enjoy anything more than an adequate access to the four necessities of life, food, shelter, clothing, and fuel, and only too likely that most men and women at some stage of life would be without some of them. The first petition in the Lord's Prayer had vivid meaning for the bulk of most congregations until the very recent past. Only in areas of new settlement where land was in plentiful supply were the necessities of life likely to be readily available throughout the population. The neolithic food revolution may have multiplied numbers as impressively as the Industrial Revolution was later to do, but it did not transform the material circumstances of the bulk of the population, though it paved the way for the appearance of extremely wealthy and powerful elites.

Clearly, if the concept of a ceiling to output consequent upon the organically based nature of material production in the pre-industrial period is acceptable, then its removal or disappearance must be an element in the understanding of the economic transformation which is commonly termed the Industrial Revolution. The classical economists were aware, of course, of the importance of technological innovation and of its increasing pace. Adam Smith had remarked on the way in which an increasing demand for new machinery and other devices to increase the scale, reduce the unit cost, and improve the quality of output was bringing into being a new type of specialist who devoted his energies to meeting this new demand.[12] But technological advance was not regarded as a promising way of overcoming the forces that would in the long term drag economies towards the stationary state. All advances that were downstream, so to speak, from the production of raw materials were powerless to ameliorate the most fundamental of the problems restricting future growth. The photosynthetic constraint was untouched or only marginally affected by human ingenuity.

Though so easy to appreciate in retrospect, the changes which were of greatest importance in overcoming the limitations of all organic economies were not readily recognized by contemporaries. The *Wealth of Nations* contains a passage in which Adam Smith forecast that industrial production would become increasingly concentrated on coalfields, but he gave as a reason that fuel is an essential part of the family budget of the labouring poor and that, since coal was a cheaper source of heat than wood, wages would be lower on coalfields than elsewhere and would therefore attract manufacture to them.[13]

The increasing use of coal, however, had an importance quite other than that to which Smith referred. Access to coal and an increasing ability to use coal in a wide variety of industrial applications meant the availability of energy on a scale an order of magnitude greater than had previously been possible, but it was the fact that coal represented a *stock* of energy that was of greatest moment. The organic economy was permanently limited to that fraction of the annual inflow of energy from the sun which was captured by photosynthesis, a part of which in turn could be secured by human ingenuity for human ends. But, since photosynthesis is an inefficient process, the *flow* of energy captured in this way could never be large enough to afford a base for an industrial economy. Wind and water power afforded a useful supplement to the energy made available through photosynthesis, but the combined total of annual energy flow deriving from insolation was an insufficient basis for an industrial revolution. The tightness of the constraints experienced by organic economies may be illustrated by the fact that, although the quantum of energy reaching the surface of Britain from the sun annually has been estimated as equivalent to 20 billion tons of coal, the inefficiency of photosynthesis as a device for converting solar energy into a form accessible to the needs of man and other animate life is such that only the equivalent of 20 million tons of coal is made available each year through photosynthesis, or a tenth of 1 per cent of the total.[14]

Coal had proved usable as a source of heat energy in England from the beginning of the early modern period, except where the problem of the transfer of chemical impurities obtruded, as with the smelting of iron. Such problems were readily perceived and gradually overcome, and when the invention and development first of the Newcomen atmospheric engine and later of Watt's more powerful and efficient improvement upon it made the steam engine an acceptable source of mechanical energy for most purposes, coal could provide an energy platform for growth on a scale which no organic economy could support. Since at the same time mineral raw materials could be refined in almost any desired quantity because coal was a cheap source of heat for smelting and working metals, other constraints inherent in organic economies were relaxed. Where output of iron had necessarily been limited to some tens, hundreds, or at the most thousands of tons, it could now rise to hundreds of thousands or even millions of tons without imposing any additional strain upon the organic cycle. Comparable relaxations applied to the production of glass, ceramics, non-ferrous metals, and later to a host of other materials.

The increasing use of coal had been a striking feature of the English economy during the seventeenth and eighteenth centuries. Throughout this period several times as much coal was produced and consumed in England as in the whole of the rest of Europe, and by the beginning of the nineteenth century English coal output had reached about 11 million tons a year, where 250 years earlier it had been only 150,000 tons.[15] To have made available the same quantity of energy by the use of wood as was being derived from coal in 1800 would have meant consuming the annual growth of wood from an area approaching half the surface area of the whole of England.[16] Since about half of the annual output of coal was put to industrial use, the extent of the dependence of industrial output at this date on an energy source that was neither animal nor vegetable is clear. Perhaps one reason why the phenomenon has attracted so little notice is that, except in the matter of mine drainage, the coal industry was far from the leading edge of technological change. The winning of coal at the coalface, its subsequent transport to the pit shaft, and its transfer to the surface all remained much as they had been for many decades. Nor is there any reason to think that output per man-hour increased to a significant degree in the two centuries before the Industrial Revolution.[17] The work was dirty, dangerous, and laborious. Coalminers, who in later years sometimes came to be referred to as the Praetorian Guard of the trade union movement, might perhaps quite as justly have been called the vanguard of the Industrial Revolution, but neither their working methods and environment nor the technology employed in coalmines suggested such prominence.

To show that a particular change was a necessary condition for an industrial revolution is not, of course, to show that its occurrence was of central importance to the explanation of the phenomenon. If it were true that the changes needed to circumvent the restrictions of an organic economy were readily achieved and might be expected to occur naturally as part of a gathering momentum of growth, then the move to a mineral-based economy using energy in very large quantities should occasion no special remark. Implicitly most accounts of the Industrial Revolution incline to this attitude. Changes in the supply of capital and labour are more likely to be treated at length than changes in the third production factor. Not that concentrating on capital and labour has quietened controversy. As empirical knowledge relating to these two factors has improved, uncertainties of interpretation have perhaps increased rather than declined.[18]

It is in this connection that the views of the classical economists are of such interest. Their treatment of the role of capital and labour in promoting economic growth has remained a starting point for discussions of the topic ever since. It is instructive, therefore, to pay attention to their reluctance to entertain great hopes for future growth. The stationary state came about not because inadequate supplies of capital were unavoidable but because there would be inadequate incentives to encourage would-be investors. Equally, they were not concerned that the supply of labour might prove insufficient, though deeply worried about the level of its future remuneration. Their pessimism stemmed from their views about the third production factor, land, and each viewed its supply as posing problems which there was no prospect of overcoming.

If their perspicacity was at fault, it was chiefly in relation to the recent history of England which provided an important example of the slackening of the restrictions associated with an organic economy, but, this apart, the rest of the history of post-neolithic but pre-industrial economies provided much support for the view of the classical economists. Several of the great civilizations of the preceding millennia had established complex and productive economies for a time, but all promising surges of growth had been followed by relapses and it was not unreasonable to see in the cycles of growth and decay exemplification of Ricardo's law of diminishing returns or of the cyclical pattern of growth and decline that Malthus's analysis of the working of the economic–demographic system had led him to expect.[19]

The classical economists did not, of course, suppose that the limitations of organic economies were the sole or even the main reason for poverty and low productivity in the past. Their exposition of the advantages of a market economy and of a capitalist system of production over the alternatives was one of their most important contributions to the establishment of political economy as a branch of human knowledge. The poverty and economic backwardness of the Turkish Empire, for example, was in Malthus's view far more a matter of the arbitrary nature of taxation, the insecurity of private property, and the impossibility of making assured calculations about the future than of any wider and more general limitations.[20] Political institutions, legal systems, property laws, and conventions of social behaviour, individually or in combination, often ensured that much growth potential was wasted and that poverty must be endemic for reasons internal to the functioning of society rather than because of other factors.

The significance of the view taken by the classical economists lies less in the direct applicability of their concept of an ultimate constraint on growth to the majority of pre-industrial economies than in their insistence that, even when a capitalist system had been established and the political and legal institutions and the attitudinal characteristics most favourable to growth were all in place, growth must still be constrained. All else being favourable, expansion could still not continue over the long term.

Assuming that it is acceptable to restate the views of the classical economists about the stationary state in terms of the limitations attaching to all organic economies, and that to escape these limitations was a necessary part of an industrial revolution, it remains to consider how to regard the escape. Was England differently placed from other economies that had experienced growth in the past, and if so, what were the differences that mattered? Can the escape be linked to some other features of the period whose presence implied that the old limitations could be circumvented? If such features existed, their significance was evidently not appreciated by the classical economists. But are they clear in hindsight?

If access to huge new *stocks* of energy were not essential to the occurrence of an industrial revolution, if the *flow* of energy available within an organic economy were capable of sustaining the transition to exponential growth from its own internal resources, then the presence or absence of mineral fuels in large quantities would not have been a matter of great moment to what was occurring in eighteenth-century England. If there had been no Carboniferous Age, no laying down of an accumulating stock of energy equivalent to untold millions of years of tree growth, in the form of coal, oil, or natural gas deposits, the Industrial Revolution would still have taken place. If, on the other hand, it is unrealistic to suppose that the use of the muscular energy of man and beast plus the fullest exploitation of wind and water power would have sufficed to sustain exponential growth, then the fact that coal was present and accessible in amounts amply sufficient to meet demand must be a necessary condition for the growth that took place.

That the use of coal rapidly transformed the outlook for economic growth in the wake of the Industrial Revolution is clear. By 1865 it seemed to Jevons that the future success of Britain in competition with rivals such as Germany, France, or the United States depended more on the comparative abundance and accessibility of their reserves of coal than upon any other single factor.[21] But it does not follow, of course, that because economies developed in this way, comparable growth with a different energy base was out of the question.

An alternative base is, however, difficult to picture. This is especially easy to specify in the case of heat energy. The traditional source of heat energy had been wood. The proportion of the land surface of England, or even of Europe, which was forest-covered was modest and could not be increased since good land was normally needed for crops or animals, and much land was too cold to grow even trees well.[22] The maximum amount of heat energy obtainable from wood was quite limited. Assuming a yield of two tons of dry timber per acre per annum implies that 1,000 square miles under woodland is unlikely to produce much more than the equivalent of about 500,000 tons of coal.[23] Given that a very substantial proportion of total timber output was needed to meet domestic fuel needs, and much more for long-established industrial needs, the balance that could be devoted to new manufactures would inevitably have been small. It is easy to see why the production of iron, even in the relatively small quantities produced during the eighteenth century by traditional means, tended to migrate to countries such as Sweden and Russia. When wood was very readily available in large quantities it continued to be used freely. It was not until after 1870 that the proportion of the total energy requirements of the United States met by wood fell below 50 per cent.[24] Standing mature timber represents perhaps a century of growth and for a time virgin forests can meet extensive fuel needs cheaply and conveniently. But the history of charcoal-fired blast furnaces in long-settled areas illustrates the difficulty of increasing output steadily without exceeding the annual timber yield of accessible land.

The link between economic growth, both in aggregate and per head, and energy consumption is close.[25] An increased consumption of energy was a normal concomitant of growth in the past as in the present. Difficulty in matching the two could be a source of difficulty and a reason for growth failing. It is arguable, for example, that the decline of Holland in the eighteenth century illustrates the point. During the Dutch golden age the production of peat soared. Though largely destitute of wood, Holland possessed large deposits of peat, some of which were readily accessible by existing waterways or through the construction of short canals with few or no locks. In the sixteenth and seventeenth centuries the output of peat was very greatly increased and peat was used both domestically and industrially on a large scale. As an energy source it bears comparison with both wood and coal in calorific value per dry ton. But Dutch peat supplies proved inadequate to meet rising needs at constant prices. The more accessible fields were largely worked out by the early eighteenth century. Failing energy supplies were not, of course, the only reason for Dutch economic difficulties in the eighteenth century, but the work of de Zeeuw suggests that the Dutch case may be instructive in showing the seriousness of the problems which afflict an economy attempting to maintain a momentum of growth if energy supplies fail or rise rapidly in price.[26]

In considering the history of economic growth in England and its culmination in the Industrial Revolution, it is important not to concentrate too heavily upon the period after, say, 1760 but to take account of relative growth rates over the whole of the early modern period as well as during the decades conventionally described as those of the Industrial Revolution. Population totals for England and the major continental countries of western Europe are known with tolerable accuracy from the middle of the sixteenth century onwards. Between 1550 and 1820 the populations of France, Germany, Italy, Spain, and the Netherlands all rose by between 50 and 80 per cent. Far less is known about changes in output per head, but if, to establish some tentative estimates of comparative growth rates, we assume that output per head increased on average by 25 per cent over this period, then aggregate output will roughly have doubled over the period. Over the same period the English population grew by about 280 per cent.[27] The extent of growth in output per head is unknown but it is probably safe to assume that it was substantially larger than in continental Europe. During this period England changed from being a relatively backward country to being the most advanced economy in Europe and most attempts to measure real incomes per head suggest that England was at this time significantly in advance of any continental country.[28] If we assume that output per head in England increased by 75 per cent in the period (probably a conservative assumption since output per head in agriculture appears to have doubled during the seventeenth and eighteenth centuries), then aggregate output will have risen six- or sevenfold.

It is arguable that a part of the very large differential between English aggregate growth and that in continental Europe is attributable to a later recovery in England than elsewhere from the huge losses of population which occurred over the century and a half following the Black Death. Yet even if some allowance is made for this, the contrast remains substantial. There was a much more marked contrast in growth rates between England and the continent in the two centuries preceding the Industrial Revolution than in the century which followed it. Indeed, by the second half of the nineteenth century several other economies were growing more rapidly than England's and the same was true of real incomes. By the end of the century her advantage had disappeared. The period of the 'classical' industrial revolution brought to an end a lengthy period of relative English success rather than instituting it.

Increasing aggregate output six or seven times implies a comparable or larger increase in energy consumption. A substantial part of this occurred because of the great strides made in increasing agricultural output. Big increases in crop yields, major reductions in the proportion of arable land kept in fallow each year, and radical changes in the range of fodder crops all imply marked success in capturing a rising proportion of the products of photosynthesis for human use.[29] This was a period when the efficiency of the organic economy was greatly increased. But it was also a period in which the use of mineral sources of energy changed still more dramatically. Coal output was negligible in the mid-sixteenth century but exceeded 10 million tons a year by the end of the eighteenth century, underwriting much of the general economic change of the period.

Many industries became partially or completely dependent upon coal – soap and salt boiling, brewing, baking, brick and tile making, glass manufacture, many aspects of the working of iron and non-ferrous metals, the heating of vats of all types, and any processes in which boiling water and steam were needed. The uses of coal ramified steadily during the seventeenth and eighteenth centuries. The scale on which London imported coal from the north-east was so great that by the Restoration about half of the entire English merchant fleet consisted of colliers plying between the Tyne or Tees and London.[30] Half of the coal produced was consumed in domestic hearths rather than in industrial use,[31] but the energy economy should be considered as a whole. The pressure on traditional sources of energy was reduced as effectively when coal was used domestically as when it was put to other uses.

The transformation of the English economy, therefore, was already far advanced by the later decades of the eighteenth century. The classical economists, and especially Smith and Malthus, who took a keen interest in recent economic history and included long digressions on the subject in their works, were well aware of the extent of the contrast between the England of, say, 1600 and the England of their own day.[32] One of their motives in writing as they did was to try to establish whether the progress that had been so evident in the past could reasonably be expected to extend into the indefinite future. Their conclusion that the stationary state would be the probable end to the present advance reflected their unconscious neglect of one important aspect of recent economic history which was progressively liberating the English economy from the negative feedback that must afflict any organically based economy at some point in its development. To sustain growth there had to be a steady rise in the production both of energy and of raw materials without sharply rising marginal production costs. The classical economists feared that it would prove impossible to secure these desiderata and further that the attempt to secure them would push any economy that pursued such aims into the pains and restrictions of the stationary state. Events were to prove them wrong, but only because the assumption that the economy would continue to be organically based turned out to be unjustified.

If the escape from the restrictions of an organic economy to the ready expansion of a mineral-based and energy-intensive mode of production had been straightforward, the change would no doubt have occurred many centuries earlier. The pains and limitations of organic economies had certainly been widely experienced. But the change was not easy to secure. Geological accident probably ruled out an easy transition in many areas. Much of the earth's surface is devoid of coal measures that were accessible to the mining technology of the pre-industrial past. The bulk of the world's coal is found in concealed coalfields where the productive strata are covered by hundreds of feet of newer rock. Nor was coal that was accessible by the mining techniques of the past capable of successful exploitation unless it outcropped close to navigable water. Land transport very soon made coal prohibitively expensive. Even in a country as small as the Netherlands some of the peat was economically inaccessible for this reason.[33]

Whether the opportunity for a gradual transfer to mineral fuel existed in many places or was very rare outside England is unclear. And the additional circumstances necessary to encourage the substitution of coal for wood would repay further attention. Conventional attitudes may have been important; coal was normally regarded as a much inferior substitute at first. In areas which might otherwise have promised well the institutional constraints to which the classical economists drew attention may often have frustrated a growth spurt. But it is likely to remain difficult to establish what might be termed the logical status of the transition that took place in England in the seventeenth and eighteenth centuries, if only because the explanation of unique events is always attended by exceptional problems.

The value of pondering on the writings of the classical economists lies in the way it reminds us that what appears to us as a gathering momentum of growth seemed to some of the ablest of contemporaries a prelude to stasis. If it is fair to see the strength of their case as springing essentially from their assessment of the limitations inherent in all organic economies and to attribute the failure of their worst fears to the progressive liberation of more and more aspects of production from the restrictions that they had assumed to be universal, then it must also be important to pay attention to the gradual strengthening of those elements in the English economy which could produce steadily rising quantities of energy and raw materials without contributing to pressure on the land. The less the country was dependent upon animal and vegetable raw materials, the less cogent was the prospect of the stationary state.

3

GREAT WAVES OF ECONOMIC CHANGE: THE INDUSTRIAL REVOLUTION IN HISTORICAL PERSPECTIVE, 1000 TO 2000[1]

Graeme Donald Snooks

A NEW PERSPECTIVE ON THE INDUSTRIAL REVOLUTION

The aim of this chapter is to discover how our interpretation of the beginning of modern economic growth changes as we alter our perspective of this fundamentally important event in the development of human society. Does the Industrial Revolution appear the same when we look forward from AD 1000 as it does when we look back, as we usually do, from the present? My concern is whether looking forward some seven centuries changes our perception of the timing of the Industrial Revolution and of the rate of growth achieved between 1760 and 1830; whether growth is a natural outcome of competitive societies or merely a modern invention; whether growth is systematic or erratic and, if systematic, through what process it is achieved; and finally, whether modern growth rates are accelerating as claimed by the 'new' growth theory.[2] To answer these questions it is necessary to place the Industrial Revolution within the context of economic change in England during the last millennium.[3]

TIME WITHOUT GROWTH?

A widely held view amongst historians, economists, and ecologists is that economic growth – defined in terms of a sustained increase in

43

GDP per capita – is a modern invention. While there are exceptions, the vast majority of scholars, both in the social and natural sciences, take it as given that rapid growth began with the Industrial Revolution, and that any growth before 1700 was very slow, and before 1500 was non-existent. The conventional wisdom tells us that economic systems in the distant past experienced, over very long periods of time, either the steady state envisaged by the classical economists, or zero-sum fluctuations in GDP per capita. According to both interpretations, ancient and medieval societies were unable to escape from poverty because they were dominated by custom rather than individual self-interest. The implications of such a conclusion are fundamental to our view of both the past and the future of the human race. Ecologists, for example, believe that just as growth was turned on at the beginning of the Industrial Revolution, so it can – indeed must – be turned off again immediately.

This view of past societies as static and disembodied is a legacy of both the liberal intellectual conviction that man aspires to higher objectives than mere material self-interest, and the ahistorical approach of economics. The argument presented here is that these interpretations continue to exist only because of the absence of quantitative data required to test them. In the absence of such data, the conviction of historians that medieval man was moral man and not economic man, and the view of classical economists that the dominating landlord class in feudal and medieval society squandered the surplus they extracted from the bulk of the population, remain largely unchallenged.[4] In this chapter an attempt will be made to estimate the change in GDP per capita over the last millennium in order to pose central questions about the nature of feudal and medieval economy, and about the role of growth in human society.[5] It will be shown not only that growth has been a persistent feature of English society over the last 1,000 years, but that it has taken place via a number of great waves of economic change.[6] The Industrial Revolution is the beginning of the last great wave.

As historians claim there are no national income data for any medieval European country or region before 1700, then they can claim no precision for their best informed guesses about the rate of economic change during the Middle Ages.[7] But because economic growth – the rise from primitive poverty and squalor – is such an important issue, a number of scholars have been tempted to speculate about the rate at which it took place over the longrun in order to provide general explanations of its progress.[8] These scholars fall into a number of categories. The first includes applied economists and historical economists such as Kuznets, Rostow, Maddison, and Persson, who use deductive reasoning, and sometimes indirect evidence, to speculate about the rate of growth of per capita income. With the exception of Persson,[9] they appear to believe that economic growth is largely a modern invention, beginning in Europe around 1500 and proceeding very slowly until the 1700s when it began to accelerate relatively rapidly for the first time. According to this interpretation, stagnation was the norm before the fifteenth century, although some speculate that zero-sum fluctuations probably occurred.[10] The clearest and most careful expression is found in Maddison, *Capitalist Development*:[11]

> For 1500–1700 the rate of progress was also very poor by present standards, but clearly better than in the previous millennium. Per capita output grew at too slow a pace to be perceptible to contemporaries . . . Nevertheless Europe's population grew by a third in these two centuries, per capita output may have risen by a quarter, and total output by around two thirds . . . Productivity rose less than income per head because the increased output required longer working hours.

Maddison, quite sensibly, takes no account of the Brown–Hopkins real wage rate index, which shows for England, France, and Alsace a substantial and sustained decline from 1500 to 1700![12] For reasons discussed later in this chapter, the Brown–Hopkins nominal wage index must be regarded as highly misleading.

The second category includes historians who are prepared to adopt an intuitive approach, such as Gould, Landes, and Komlos.[13] Gould, for example, is convinced by the apparent logic of the argument that 'it is impossible that the long-run growth rates over the last century should have been sustained for long periods prior to the mid-nineteenth century',[14] but he is also aware of the existence of partial quantitative evidence on economic change in the Middle Ages (unfortunately evidence such as Brown–Hopkins[15]). Sensibly, Gould suggests that this historical evidence is consistent 'with the hypothesis that the period of modern economic growth was preceded by marked secular fluctuations of real income, impressive improvements being cancelled by later and equally impressive declines, *rather* than with the alternative . . . namely . . . centuries-long stagnation or growth at a rate infinitesimally above zero'. But, as I will demonstrate, this view is based upon the entirely misleading real wage index of Brown and Hopkins. More recently, other historians, such as Komlos,[16] who does not refer to the work of Brown and Hopkins or Gould, have re-emphasized in a speculative and non-empirical way the possibility of secular swings within the context of 'thousands of years of very slow economic growth'. Landes begins from a position similar to that of Gould by claiming:[17]

> We have no true statistical estimates of pre-modern growth; but one has only to extrapolate the levels of income prevalent on the eve of industrialization backward at the rates of growth prevailing after 1700, and one arrives very quickly at levels of income too low for human survival.

He also acknowledges that there were major periods of economic downturn such as the century or so after the Black Death and periodic Malthusian crises. In view of this dismal scenario it is surprising that his informed guess about the growth of per capita income is more optimistic than Gould's: 'Even so,' Landes concludes, 'it seems clear that over the near-millennium from the year 1000 to the eighteenth century, income per head rose appreciably – perhaps tripled – and that this rise accelerated sharply in the eighteenth century, even before the introduction of the new industrial technology.' Later in this chapter I suggest that while the logic employed by this group of scholars cannot be faulted, their arguments are based upon faulty assumptions.

The final category includes scholars like Pollard, Crossley, Clarkson, Cipolla, Jones, and Wrigley, who attempt to build up a general picture of changes in wealth and income by examining more indirect, and generally non-quantitative, evidence. Jones, for example, claims in his more recent work that 'prolonged high rates of growth are not to be found until the Europe of the eighteenth or nineteenth centuries';[18] and that before 1700 growth took place at 'a permanently low rate' which 'asks too much of the usual models. It happens too gradually and over too long a span.'[19] Extending his focus to the whole world over the two or three millennia before 1800, Jones writes: 'The world economy as a whole seems not to have grown in the per capita income sense. On the other hand, population growth and technical change did impart a momentum of continual expansion.'[20] His view, therefore, is that before the Industrial Revolution slow economic expansion (an increase in population with the same level of per capita income) was not uncommon, particularly in Europe, but that economic growth (an increase in per capita income) rarely broke free from the political constraints that confined it to very low positive (or negative) rates. The exceptions that Jones feels confident in nominating are China in the tenth to thirteenth centuries, Japan 1600 to 1868, and Europe 1500 to 1800 (interestingly, like Maddison, this contradicts the real wage rate indexes of Brown and Hopkins); and even these exceptions have only appeared in his more recent work,[21] possibly under the influence of the historical economists. From his earlier work[22] one has the impression that he initially believed that significant sustained growth in per capita income was not experienced anywhere in the world, including Europe, before the late sixteenth century. While Jones is to be credited with raising recent interest in the issue of very longrun change, it appears reasonable to conclude that he does not see economic growth as either systematic or rising above zero-sum fluctuations for the pre-modern period. Finally, Tony Wrigley says: 'During the nineteenth century economic growth rates rose to levels far higher than had ever been consistently attained previously . . .'.[23]

There is, therefore, little agreement in detail about the possible magnitude of longrun growth rates, which is hardly surprising in the absence of any previous attempt to marshal the national income data required to calculate them. With the possible exceptions of Landes and Persson, however, most of the scholars who have speculated about this matter appear to believe that growth rates of per capita income in Europe were very slow before 1700 and largely non-existent before 1500. Many of these scholars recognize that although growth throughout the millennium before 1700 may not have been significantly different to zero, there were periods of improvement that were largely cancelled out by periods of regression. The exception is Jones who, if I have interpreted him correctly, implies that growth occurred not in terms of systematic economic cycles in individual countries or regions but rather by breaking out almost randomly for political reasons on relatively rare occasions in various parts of the world, possibly never (at least in the pre-1700 period) to occur there again.

The results in this chapter challenge the conventional wisdom that the longrun rate of economic growth in Europe was very slow before 1700, and non-existent before 1500. They also challenge the view that growth was a result not of systematic economic forces, but of political processes, and suggest that the generalized explanations (largely inductive models) that have been developed to explain economic change (or its absence) are highly sensitive to the *assumed* pattern and rate of growth. Instead it is argued that growth in England – and by implication Europe – was relatively rapid, sustained, systematic, and that it occurred through the generation of great waves of change that are surging from the past and into the future.

LONGRUN POPULATION GROWTH

The contours of population growth in England, which are reasonably reliably known, can be employed as a first approximation to an examination of economic expansion during the last millennium. While fairly complete population censuses did not begin until 1801, plausible estimates of population by Wrigley and Schofield, based upon demographic data contained within parish records, are available back to 1541.[24] Before this time only approximate estimates are available for the widely scattered individual years of 1525 (based upon tax returns and muster certificates), 1450 (manorial records and indirect evidence), 1377 (poll tax and a sample of manors), 1347 (sample of manors), and 1086 (Domesday Book).[25] Of the medieval estimates, the most reliable is that for 1086, which is based upon the comprehensive Domesday survey.

From Figure 3.1 it can be seen that the population of England, which increased by a factor of 33.1 from 1.53 million in 1086 to 50.7 million in 1990, experienced three main periods of longrun expansion during this millennium. The first was from Domesday to the Black Death – a period of 261 years; the second from the Tudor revival to Oliver Cromwell – a period of 125 years; and the third, from the Industrial Revolution until the late 1960s – a period of 220 years. Of these the first and third were quite similar in terms of length – in excess of two centuries – and in terms of the rate of population growth (see the slopes of the population curves in Figure 3.1), although the second occurred slightly more rapidly than the first. Population growth during the sixteenth and seventeenth centuries – the middle period – was quite rapid, but was brought to a close during the 1650s, by which time the pre–Black Death population level had just been re-attained, after a lapse of three centuries. This long downswing in population is the most remarkable feature of Figure 3.1. The second pause in the expansion of population, from 1650 to 1750, is only a shallow and short-lived depression in comparison, as probably will be the levelling off in the last quarter of the twentieth century.

Population, of course, is only part of the story of economic change. We also need to know how the population's average living standards

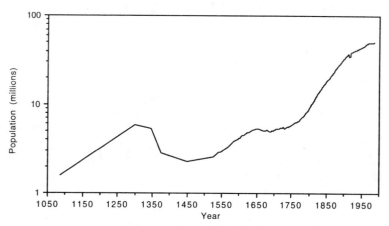

Figure 3.1 The population of England, 1086–1990
Note: Log scale on vertical axis
Sources: See text and Snooks, *Economics without Time*, ch. 7

changed over the same period of time. The most coherent view of economic historians on this issue is that there was an inverse relationship between population and average living standards.[26] This view is based upon use of Brown and Hopkins' real wage rate index for building workers around Oxford. There are, however, a number of fundamental practical and conceptual problems involved in using this index as a proxy for living standards in England. First, the nominal wage data are highly suspect in the Middle Ages because of the rudimentary and local nature of labour markets, the small and unrepresentative sample, and the fact that it consists of piece rates rather than wage rates. Secondly, even if the index is representative of the entire building industry, it is not necessarily representative of wage rates for all occupations and, even if it were, this would not make it a good proxy for average living standards of the peasant/working class let alone the entire population. This is particularly so in an economy where the landowning class was able to extract such a large proportion of the total surplus. Both the secular trend and the fluctuations are contradicted by other evidence. And there are good reasons, mainly concerning the nominal wages component, to doubt that the Brown–Hopkins index is a reliable *longrun* measure of even the real wage rates of building workers in Oxford. There is, therefore, good reason to estimate directly the growth of GDP per capita over the last millennium.

ESTIMATING MILLENNIAL GROWTH RATES

Domesday Book provides a new starting point for the estimation of English growth. The year 1086 is almost exactly 600 years prior to Gregory King's national income estimates which have for long been wrongly regarded as the earliest relatively reliable macroeconomic data. During the intervening period between Domesday Book and Gregory King, which for the quantitative economic historian is largely shrouded in a mist of obscurity, the economic system of England was transformed from a feudal manorial economy to a mercantile capitalist economy that was on the threshold of a structural transformation later known as the Industrial Revolution. What did this great institutional (or, more accurately, systems) change bring with it in terms of material economic growth? We cannot precisely chart the changes from year to year, or even from generation to generation, but we can evaluate the magnitude of change in material well-being over the entire period of six hundred years by using Domesday Book to reconstruct the national income of England in 1086 and compare it with the estimates of Gregory King in 1688.[27]

The national income of Domesday England

As I have discussed my estimates of Domesday national income in detail elsewhere, they will be dealt with only briefly here.[28] But before turning to the data we must consider the nature of the Domesday economy. The overriding objectives of the manorial economy of Domesday England were to produce a surplus that could be employed: to provide a fully equipped feudal army to secure the country against invasion; to satisfy a warrior king's desire for further wealth and power through conquest; and to meet the consumption and investment demands of the ruling elite. Not surprisingly, the surplus, which was known as the *valet*, was given pride of place in Domesday Book. The *valet* is the basic building block in my estimate of national income.

The manorial system consisted of two parts – the demesne economy which provided the manorial lord and free peasant with a surplus, and the subsistence economy which sustained the *unfree* labour that worked on the demesne. It is essential to realize that the income of free peasants, who lived somewhat above subsistence level in all but the worst years, is recorded in Domesday Book in the annual values, and hence is included as part of the demesne economy. Only unfree peasants are included in the subsistence sector. This was a dependent form of agriculture in which bonded or unfree peasants worked on the lord's demesne in return for land and capital that were just sufficient to maintain them and their families at the minimum consumption level *that would ensure the maximization of the manorial surplus* and a steady growth of population. In 1086 this approached physiological subsistence, and even in the fourteenth century scholars talk of the 'knife edge of subsistence' and the 'peasant art of starvation'.[29] The lord was able to enforce this one-sided contract on his dependent peasant workforce, despite the fact that labour rather than land was the scarce factor of production, because of his military monopoly and the monopsony arrangement with his fellow barons and knights. In the process the manorial lord was able to maximize the economic rent he could extract from labour. The economic position of the bonded peasant, as far as the lord was concerned, was little different to that of the plough beasts – the surpluses over and above the costs of maintaining labour and capital (in both cases food and shelter) were extracted through the manorial system.

This form of economic management is consistent with my argument elsewhere that manorial lords were economically rational.[30] The manorial system was a form of dependent agriculture precisely because labour was the scarce factor of production, and the only alternative to the threat of force, both military and ecclesiastical, by manorial lords was competition between them. The latter, which would have increased the return to labour and reduced the manorial surplus, would not have been a rational undertaking by manorial lords within the economic circumstances of the late eleventh century. Also the threat of force was an effective method of surplus extraction, because its use was largely costless to manorial lords in a society geared up for war, because the manorial system was capable of close supervision thereby minimizing shirking, and because the need to survive provided peasants with an incentive to complete their work on the demesne as quickly and as effectively as possible so as to be released to work on their own land.

The surplus generated by the manorial system is recorded in Domesday Book as the 'annual values' (*valets*). This surplus can be thought of as gross manorial production on all land encompassed by the manor minus intermediate goods (such as grain seed) and those goods produced on the manor (such as fodder and rough shelter for livestock; food, clothing, and shelter for slaves; and the subsistence output of the peasants' land) in order to maintain manorial resources.

51

This is, of course, equivalent to the microeconomic definition of value-added. To put it another way, the annual value is the return to the manorial lord from owning or controlling the resources of the manor, and it includes a return for risk, together with economic rents and quasi-rents extracted from factors that were scarce or in fixed supply in the shortrun. To translate this microeconomic concept of value-added into modern national income terms, the usual convention has been followed of adding back into 'value-added' the cost of maintaining human labour. Accordingly, the manorial component of national income in 1086 must include not only the demesne income (or the annual values) but also unfree peasant subsistence income (see Table 3.1).

Table 3.1 The national income of feudal England, 1086

National Income	
Manorial Income (£)	
Recorded counties	
demesne economy	71,573
subsistence economy	51,306
Omitted counties	3,034
Burghal Income	10,708
Total	136,621
Per Capita Income (shillings)	1.785

Note: Non-recorded income estimated on the assumption that the average household size was 5.0 people, and that slaves were recorded in the same way as the rest of the population (i.e. as household heads)
Sources and methods: See text; Snooks, 'Last millennium'; and Snooks, *Economics without Time*, ch. 5

Manorial income – the demesne economy

The total value of demesne income, which includes that for all manorial lords and free peasants, can be obtained from Domesday Book by aggregating the annual values for some 40,000 rural holdings. The underlying data and method are far more reliable and robust than those used by Gregory King – basically estimates of numbers of families and estimates of average family income – some six hundred years later. But there are marginal adjustments that must be made to the aggregated total of annual values (or domestic income) for rural holdings in Domesday Book to cover a number of relatively small omissions. These omissions include the four most northern English counties, and the urban centres which included about 8 per cent of the population in 1086.

As the detailed task of aggregating the annual values, or demesne income, requires the exercise of value judgements owing to the problem of allocating individual manors within estates to particular counties, the totals obtained by different scholars will always be *slightly* different. The totals obtained by Maitland and Darby differ by £264, or 0.37 per cent. Such minor discrepancies, which make no significant difference to estimates of per capita income, can be safely ignored. In this study Darby's carefully aggregated total of £71,573 for demesne income has been adopted.[31]

Manorial income – the unfree peasant subsistence economy

The subsistence sector (which includes only unfree peasants) involved a mix of agricultural and non-agricultural activities, which were reflected in the variation of individual economic 'responsibilities' (days of work on the lord's demesne) and 'rights' (land use). This in turn suggests that we can think of the subsistence sector as a 'closed' economy in which there is a degree of economic specialization and exchange, with the only constraint being that the total amount of land and capital allocated by the manorial lord is sufficient to sustain the bonded peasant population. Domesday Book, however, does not allow a direct calculation of the value or structure of subsistence output, precisely because it did not provide a taxable surplus. But the Conqueror's great survey does provide sufficient information to enable a calculation of the net output required to maintain the unfree labour force – the villeins, bordars, cottars, etc., and slaves – at a level which enabled manorial lords to maximize their incomes. And it contains income data for the holdings of small free peasants that can be used to check my estimate of per capita subsistence income for the unfree peasants (the former is only 16 per cent greater than the latter). As already discussed, the consumption level of unfree peasants is thought to have approached physiological subsistence in the late eleventh century. What is required, therefore, is an estimate of the value of the subsistence requirements of bonded peasants and their families in terms of food, clothing, and shelter. This estimate is a viable alternative – but only before the twelfth century, after which retained surpluses for formerly bonded peasants began to emerge – to the usual method of calculating the total net output of land (of which we have no record) allocated by manorial lords to their bonded peasants. The major component of subsistence income is food. An estimate of the value of food consumption can be undertaken by: reconstructing the structure of the average Domesday peasant household; estimating the expected energy requirements of that household; and calculating the cost of meeting those requirements. To this I have added a mark-up of 10 per cent to cover the cost of clothing, housing, and heating, all of which were very primitive.[32] The final estimates of national income in England in 1086 are presented in Table 3.1.

From Domesday Book to Gregory King

An estimate of GDP per capita for England in 1086 is presented in Table 3.2. The next year for which we have a reasonably reliable estimate of GDP per capita is 1688, calculated by Gregory King. As much excellent work has been undertaken on King's accounts, only a brief discussion is required here. The first point to note is that the estimate by King, whether reworked by Deane or Lindert and Williamson, is not as firmly based as that for 1086.[33] Others have adequately detailed the problems with King's work.[34] Nevertheless, when appropriately adjusted, it is widely regarded as providing a relatively reliable basis for measuring the rate of economic progress during the eighteenth century. Even Crafts, despite his words of caution, is prepared to exploit it in his work.[35] Also the remarkably consistent and plausible econometric results obtained recently by Sir Richard Stone from his estimation of tax and consumption functions using King's estimates suggest that the data are more reliable than

Table 3.2 The economic condition of England, 1086 and 1688

Year	National income Nominal prices (£m)	1688 prices (£m)	Population (000s)	Rural h/hold heads (000s)	Price (1688=100)	Real per capita income (£)	Real per h/hold income (£)
1086	0.137	2.63	1,531	275	5.2	1.72	9.55
1688	50.800	50.80	5,136	1,300	100.0	9.89	39.08

Note: Wales has been excluded from the 1688 total on a per capita basis. The 1801 census was used to calculate the ratio of population between England and Wales, and this was applied to King's estimate of 5.5 million

Sources: 1086: See text and Snooks, *Economics without Time*, ch. 5
      1688: National income: Lindert and Williamson, 'England's social tables', p.389
Population and prices: Snooks, *Economics without Time*, ch. 5.

some commentators have been prepared to admit.[36] Hence I have accepted King's calculations of national income, population, and per capita income for England and Wales as adjusted by Lindert and Williamson. Secondly, in order to make a comparison of national income between 1086 and 1688 it is necessary to exclude the national income of Wales in the latter year because Domesday Book did not include the subdued but unconquered Welsh tribes. This can be achieved in an approximate way for 1688 by applying the per capita income of England and Wales to the Welsh population and subtracting this subtotal from King's aggregate. Obviously, this procedure leaves per capita income unchanged. Thirdly, it should be noted that as royal revenues are included in the 1086 national income figure but excluded in 1688, the resulting growth rate calculation will be an underestimate. The current price estimates have been expressed in 1688 prices by constructing a weighted price index using the prices of household consumables and the prices of wheat.[37]

The GDP per capita results are presented in Table 3.2. As one would expect, the differences in the economic condition of England between 1086 and 1688 are striking. The productive capability of the economy had been transformed, even before the impact of the Industrial Revolution. Real national income increased by an unexpectedly high factor of 19.3; population by a relatively small factor of 3.4; prices by a factor of 19.2; real per capita income – the measure of economic growth – by a surprisingly high factor of 5.8; and real per household income – a rough measure of labour productivity – by a factor of 4.1. Clearly, the transformation of the English economy during those six centuries was far higher than even the most optimistic historians have been prepared to suggest. And the implication of the magnitude of these results is that the economy made considerable permanent gains in per capita income between 1000 and 1500, as well as between 1500 and 1700. These results will require a radical reinterpretation of economic change in England and Europe during the last millennium.

THE NATURE OF MILLENNIAL GROWTH

Growth during the Middle Ages and the modern era

Economic growth during the six centuries prior to 1700 occurred at a relatively high rate – in the vicinity of 0.3 per cent per annum (Table 3.3). This unexpectedly high figure implies that, on average, real per capita income was compounded by 34 per cent each century or, to put it another way, by 8 per cent every generation (of twenty-five years). Quite clearly, this is a change that would have been perceived by individuals, some of whom lived out their 'three score years and ten', and by families which possessed even longer memories. Further, it will be shown that there were periods during these six centuries when growth rates were three to six times higher than the average. Therefore, despite the claims of many historians – both quantitative and non-quantitative – medieval populations were keenly aware of economic change, favourable as well as unfavourable.

Table 3.3 Growth rates for England, 1086–1688 (percentages)

	National income (1688 prices)	Per capita income (1688 prices)	Rural household income (1688 prices)	Population	Prices
Per annum	0.49	0.29	0.23	0.20	0.49
Per generation	13.13	7.56	6.15	5.17	13.11
Per century	63.80	33.85	26.47	22.35	63.68

Note: A generation is taken to be 25 years
Source: See text and Snooks, *Economics without Time*, ch. 7

But how does growth during the Middle Ages compare with modern growth that began with the Industrial Revolution? Table 3.4 indicates that the average rate of growth of GDP per capita for the 600 years before 1688 was almost the same as that for the first half of the eighteenth century, and as much as 83 per cent of that in the second half of the century. In other words, *growth rates during the first half of the Industrial Revolution were only marginally higher*

Table 3.4 Growth rates for England, 1086–1987 (real per capita income)

Period	% pa	Period	% pa
1086–1688	0.29	1830–1870	1.4
1688–1760	0.31	1870–1913	1.0
1760–1780	0.01	1913–1950	0.8
1780–1801	0.35	1950–1973	2.5
1801–1831	0.52	1973–1987	1.5

Sources: 1086–1688: See text and Snooks, *Economics without Time*, ch. 7
1688–1831: Crafts, *British Economic Growth*, p. 45
1830–1987: Maddison, *Capitalist Development*, p. 6

than the average achieved for the previous six hundred years. Even during the latter stages of the Industrial Revolution (1801–1837), the 600 year average was not disgraced – it was as high as 61 per cent of the former. Of course this comparison between the Middle Ages and the Industrial Revolution is based upon an average rate of growth over six centuries. As we know there were prolonged periods of slump – such as the long decline between 1300 and 1450, when growth rates were negative or only barely positive – rates of growth during the long upswings – such as 1000 to 1300 and 1500 to 1620 – must have been considerably higher than 0.3 per cent per annum. Estimates based upon the simulated reconstruction in Figure 3.3 and presented in Table 3.5 suggest that growth rates from 1086 to 1170 were in the vicinity of 0.6 per cent per annum and those between 1492 and 1600 were approximately 1.3 per cent per annum, and even rose to 1.6 per cent per annum between 1492 and 1560. As can be seen from Table 3.4, this compares favourably with British growth rates achieved in the nineteenth and twentieth centuries. While the growth rate of the sixteenth century was enhanced by the reaction of the English economy to a sudden release from the grip of pestilence, so too the growth rate of the mid-twentieth century was enhanced by a sudden release from the grip of world war. We can conclude, therefore, that the growth record of the Industrial Revolution, and even that of the last two centuries, was not at all remarkable in terms of past experience.

Table 3.5 Approximate growth rates, England, 1086–1688

Period	% p.a.	Period	% p.a.
1086–1170	0.6	1372–1491	0.1
1171–1280	0.2	1492–1561	1.6
1281–1301	0.02	1562–1601	0.8
1302–1371	−0.7	1602–1688	0.1

Source: See text and Snooks, *Economics without Time*, ch. 7

Many authors, on the basis of comparative analysis of modern economies have suggested that the uniqueness of the British Industrial Revolution lies not in the rate of growth, but rather in three distinguishing characteristics: structural change, technological change, and the initiation of a system of self-sustaining growth. This longrun analysis of the growth of England suggests that there is some truth in this claim, but it also suggests that certain qualifications should be noted. First, economic development during the six centuries preceding the Industrial Revolution was not without structural change. In 1086 urban population as a proportion of total population was about 8 per cent, whereas by the early eighteenth century this sector had increased by a factor of 2.5 to include as much as 15 per cent of the population.[38] Considerable structural change, therefore, had occurred prior to the Industrial Revolution. The uniqueness of the Industrial Revolution was the speed at which this structural change took place. The second claim about technological change must also be qualified. Major new techniques were introduced into agriculture (water mills, windmills, irrigation works, field rotations, horses rather than oxen, etc.), mining, and transport and communications throughout the Middle Ages.[39] But it may well be true that technological change was not as important as organizational change in the Middle Ages. The third claim is clearly wrong, as sustained economic growth, even for as long as three centuries, was a major characteristic of pre-modern societies. Economic growth is definitely not a modern invention.

How was it possible to achieve such high growth rates?

Most scholars have found it difficult to envisage rates of growth of per capita income as high as the estimates in this chapter. This is because they have failed to draw a distinction between the consumption of perishables on the one hand and of the services of durables on the other, and because they have not recognized that growth in the very longrun proceeds via great waves of economic change.

First, there obviously is a limit to reductions in the level of food, clothing, and shelter, and that is the level of physiological subsistence. In 1086 the bulk of the population was close to that level,[40] as they had always been, and from time to time many were plunged below it owing to widespread harvest failures resulting from natural (floods, droughts and disease) or man-made causes (invasion, war, reprisals), which laid the land waste – a term often invoked in the Domesday record for the northern and western counties. But it was a level that was no worse than that experienced in India during the mid-nineteenth century.[41] By 1688, the margin between bare subsistence and the average consumption level was greater,[42] although not by a multiple of six.

The major improvement over these six centuries was in terms of the consumption of services arising from a vastly improved physical environment in the form of better housing (from, on average, rough shelters often shared with livestock to more substantial, durable, comfortable, and dignified structures); better village and urban facilities (social, health, educational, as well as economic); better transport and communication facilities, which reduced isolation; and better facilities for storing and transporting food, thereby reducing the impact of disasters. The available evidence (see Table 3.6) suggests that the per capita consumption of perishables increased by a factor of three – which may have been largely due to the expansion of the middle class rather than a significant improvement in the consumption standards of the mass of the population – and that the remaining part of per capita income increased by a factor of nineteen. It is the difference in rates of change of the various components of national income that Gould,[43] for example, overlooked.[44] Also it is probably for this reason that Landes' guesstimate of growth[45] is only one-half of my calculation of the growth of per capita income, but equal to my estimate of the per capita growth of the consumption of perishables. None of this implies, however, that there was no growth before 1086; earlier long-term growth resulted not in an increase in living standards of the masses, but in an increase in the surplus of the relatively small but powerful elite. The remarkable redistribution of GDP per capita from a small elite to the great mass of the population in developed societies is the unique achievement of the modern phase of economic growth initiated by the Industrial Revolution.

Table 3.6 Components of per capita income, 1086 and 1688

	$\dfrac{Cp}{Y}$	$\dfrac{Y}{P}$	$\dfrac{Cp}{P}$	$\dfrac{Y-Cp}{P}$
1086	0.86	£1.72	£1.48	£0.24
1688	0.50	£9.89	£4.45	£4.45
Factor increase	–	5.8	3.0	18.5

Note: Cp = consumption of perishables, Y = national income, P = population
Sources: The Cp/Y ratios from text and King, *Two Tracts*; and Y/P estimates from text. See Snooks, *Economics without Time*, chs 5 and 7

Secondly, the longrun average of 0.3 per cent per annum for the 600 years prior to 1700 masks shorter-term fluctuations that are more violent than anything experienced in England in the modern period (although not more violent than in Germany or the USSR in this century) because of the force of the exogenous shocks. As we have seen, growth rates during the period 1000 to 1200 compare favourably with those during the Industrial Revolution, and the rates achieved in the sixteenth century (see Table 3.5) are as impressive as those in the nineteenth and twentieth centuries. It is highly likely that the rates in the first half of the sixteenth century are higher than those before the Black Death in part as a reaction to the negative rates (−0.7 per cent per annum) between 1302 and 1371, and very slow growth (0.1 per cent per annum) between 1372 and 1491, experienced as a result of the shock of the Black Death and the century and a half of pestilence and war that followed. Partly for the same reason, the 1950s and 1960s appear just as atypical in the modern era as the sixteenth century seems in the pre-modern age.

Growth rates of this magnitude for the later Middle Ages and early modern period should not have come as such a surprise, as there is ample evidence that the surplus over and above consumption requirements was growing significantly during the six centuries after the Conquest. First, there is extensive archaeological evidence, particularly for the periods 1000–1300 and 1490–1620, concerning the growing capital intensity of infrastructure (or capital deepening) in villages, towns, ports, together with that of the expanding transport facilities, as well as an increase in capital widening with a population that increased from 1.5 to 5.5 million.[46] Secondly, many scholars have emphasized the steady advance of technology during these six centuries.[47] Thirdly, while the expansion of Europe into the rest of the world throughout this period was facilitated by the technical advances occurring in transport and navigation, it relied upon the growth of surpluses over and above consumption requirements. Phillips, for example, has shown that between 1000 and 1500 European influence extended to Greenland, Iceland, north America, the eastern Mediterranean, Cyprus, the 'Latin Empire' of Constantinople, and west Africa; and after 1500 there was a large-scale conquest of the Americas involving the migration of Europeans on an unprecedented scale.[48] Fourthly, these growth rates are consistent with the recent findings that the English economy of the eleventh century, being open to market forces, was economically rational, dynamic, flexible, and enterprising – in short capable of generating sustained economic growth.[49]

Finally, and unfortunately, the potentially important evidence on population heights in the very longrun is, as yet, too incomplete to enable us to draw any conclusions. Of course, it could not be employed as evidence for changes in per capita income, but it could theoretically tell us something about changing levels of the per capita consumption of perishables. But to do this it must be representative of the various socio-economic groups in England. It is to be expected, for example, that the very marked difference in nutritional status between the manorial lords, the free peasants, and the unfree peasants and slaves would lead to a significant difference in average heights between these groups. We would also need to know how long they had been members of the social class in which they died – were they English earls reduced to serfdom or French peasants raised to the aristocracy through valour in battle? The present data on heights for the late Anglo-Saxon period, obtained from the excavation of burial sites, are available in very small numbers (only 78 observations between 850 and 1086, and 174 observations over the thirteenth and fourteenth centuries), are thinly scattered over these periods of time, and are not identified by socio-economic status. Indeed, it is completely misleading to assemble these data in tabular form, even when the deficiencies are carefully recited.[50]

The sources of growth during the Middle Ages

Although further research is required, particularly concerning changes in capital stock, it is possible at this stage to reach tentative conclusions about the well springs of pre-modern growth. Table 3.3 shows that the rate of growth of population (0.20 per cent per annum) was only 41 per cent of the rate of growth of real national income (0.49 per cent per annum) and 69 per cent of the rate of growth of real per capita income (0.29 per cent per annum). In other words, while the contribution of population to the increase in real national income, and hence to economic development, was important, it was only two-thirds as important as the contribution of non-population forces (as reflected in the growth of per capita income) such as the growth of capital stock (both physical and human), technological change, economies of scale, and reduction in transactions costs associated with the transition of the English economy from feudalism to mercantile capitalism. The longrun average relationship between the growth of both population and GDP per capita is shown graphically for the last millennium in Figure 3.2. What is interesting here is the contrast in this relationship between the periods of modern and pre-modern growth. From 1086 to 1688, the rate of growth of GDP per capita was slightly higher than that of population, but after 1688 this relationship was reversed, at least until after the Second World War, with population growing at a significantly faster rate than GDP per capita. This suggests that during the process of modern growth the trade-off between the increase in population and the improvement in average living standards shifted towards the former. What this appears to mean is that modern growth generated a more equitable distribution of income, by transferring a higher proportion of the national surplus from the 'ruling elite' to the 'working class', thereby enabling a population to grow at the expense of the living standards not of the working class but of the ruling elite. This could have resulted from a transfer of the national surplus between social groups with significantly different average propensities (from a lower to a higher level) to consume.

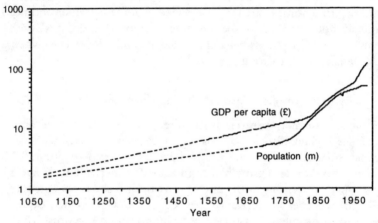

Figure 3.2 The longrun growth of population and GDP per capita, England, 1086–1990

Notes: The curves between 1086 and 1688 are based upon average rates of change
Log scale on vertical axis
Sources: See text and Snooks, *Economics without Time*, ch. 7

This is a fundamentally important conclusion, because it has major implications for the way we view the nature of economic expansion and growth in the pre-industrial period – a period that encompasses most of human experience. It is important for at least two reasons. First, it challenges the overly strong emphasis often placed upon population growth as the dynamic driving force behind economic development during the last millennium.[51] The problem with these intuitive theories is that they are not based upon empirical investigation – no attempt has been made to quantify either the rate of economic change or the contribution of the main sources of development – and tend to be models in search of accommodating events. The empirical results in this chapter suggest that, although population growth may have acted to initiate and terminate 'shorter' surges (even of a century or so in duration) of economic expansion, its direct contribution to longrun economic development during the Middle Ages was not as great as many have claimed. This is not, however, to belittle its achievement. But the great economic achievement – and it was great – of the six centuries before the Industrial Revolution was not just a more widespread and intensive colonization of England (although that did occur), rather it was a more efficient use of its natural and labour resources. This conclusion appears particularly robust because, if anything, I have underestimated the GDP per capita growth rate.

The second, and related, reason for the importance of these results is that it focuses our attention on the forces influencing the growth of productivity. These forces are major players in our drama. The educated guess made by historical economists[52] that any growth that did occur between 1500 and 1700 was largely the result of a reduction in underemployment is not supported by the results in this chapter (Table 3.3) which show that labour productivity growth (column 3 is a proxy for GDP per unit of labour) was as high as 80 per cent of economic growth from 1086 to 1688. We need to ask – although I will not be able to answer it fully here – what accounted for the amazing increase in labour productivity. Modern economists normally think of productivity advances in terms of changes in technology, economies of scale, and the quality of factors of production. Although these forces are important, this approach is limited because it employs the growth accounting approach which is based upon a comparative static production function model.[53] That approach, by ignoring time, assumes that institutional arrangements are basically static. More recently, some historical economists, namely North and Thomas, have attempted to move the debate beyond the timeless analytical approach of modern economics by considering the longrun growth implications of institutional change.[54] While this has been an important contribution, the emphasis of their work seems to exclude longrun changes in human and physical capital accumulation and those narrowly economic forces driving productivity change; and like all the other studies of this topic it lacks a clear empirical focus, and thereby shares the disembodied nature of the genre. The transformation of Europe from a feudal (or proto-feudal) economy to a mercantile capitalist system greatly improved the efficiency of economic relationships within and between countries as markets evolved further and transactions costs were reduced.[55] At the same time there was a steady increase in human skills and physical capital stock (particularly in transport and communication) and a build-up of appropriate technology, all of which was necessary to support the fundamental changes taking place in England's economic system. Although this must be thought of as a highly integrated process of institutional, physical, and intellectual change, we need to emphasize the importance of the institutional base that economists treat as given.[56] An attempt will be made to give some empirical content to this story in future work.

Non-quantitative economic historians – such as Landes, Gould, and Jones – have also emphasized the role of technological change. Jones, for example, has focused upon long-term 'technological drift', which he views as being a function not of economic forces, but of a psychological will to innovate. This obsession to innovate, which because of its alleged pervasiveness apparently requires no economic explanation, is like a spring bubbling constantly to the surface that only fails to nourish economic growth because it is diverted into non-economic uses by an oppressive class of 'arbitrary' warlords. Only once the 'arbitrary' intervention of powerful ruling elites is overcome, by political rather than economic forces, does the upwelling of the will to innovate become translated into an increase in per capita income, which will be reversed if there is a change in the political climate. To my mind, there are many problems with the type of explanation that makes an appeal to non-economic and largely unanalysed forces, not least of which is the fact that there is abundant evidence to show that feudal, and pre-feudal, warlords did *not* act in arbitrary, and hence economically irrational, ways.[57] Also the structure of inductive models of this type is highly sensitive to the *assumed* rate of growth which, as we have seen, is certainly not valid for England, and is probably not valid for western Europe, over the last millennium.

GREAT WAVES OF ECONOMIC CHANGE, AD 1000–2000

It seems quite clear from the above examination of changes in population and average living standards that the growth process of the English economy passed through a number of long upswings or, as they are called here, great waves of economic change. A computer simulated representation of these great waves for the period 1086 to 1688, which is based upon changes in population, GDP, and GDP per capita, is presented in Figure 3.3. Although this figure has been reconstructed carefully from detailed data concerning the trend, amplitude, and shape of the fluctuations in these macroeconomic variables, it makes no claims for precision in the shorter term.[58] Roughly speaking the great waves of growth and expansion over the last millennium appear to be three in number: 1000 to 1300, 1490 to 1620, and the 1700s to the 1990s. Each of these upswings was both rapid and prolonged. The first and the third upswings took about 300 years to work themselves out, while the second, which was largely conditioned by an earlier century or so of demographic and military disruption, came to an end after 130 years. As Figure 3.3 shows, these episodes of growth coincide closely with sustained increases in wheat prices, which not only provides greater confidence in the simulated real GDP and GDP per capita results (as they were not part of the simulation procedure), but also suggests that the driving forces behind these great waves are to be found on the demand side. In the absence of the massive exogenous shocks of the fourteenth and

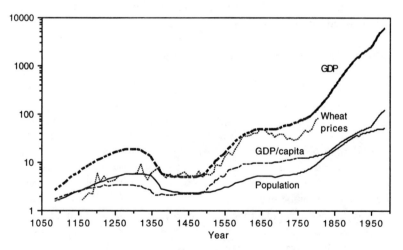

Figure 3.3 Great waves of economic change in England during the last millennium

Notes: Log scale on vertical axis; for units of measurement see Appendix
Source: See Appendix (Table 3.7) and Snooks, *Economics without Time*, ch. 7
© G.D. Snooks, RSSS, ANU, 1991

65

fifteenth centuries, it is possible that the middle wave would also have been of approximately 300 years duration. But while the evidence supports great waves of a systematic nature, it would be purely coincidental if they were also regular in duration.

Some independent confirmation of the timing and duration of these great waves is provided by evidence on changing patterns of longevity. Existing research into the life expectancy of males at birth (in non-epidemic periods) suggests that it rose from about 28 years in the mid-eleventh century, to 33 years in the early fifteenth century, to 42 years by the end of the sixteenth century, to 47 years by the late nineteenth century, to over 60 years by the 1930s, and to over 70 years by the 1990s.[59] In other words, there was a modest increase (18 per cent) between 1086 and 1300, a more substantial increase (27 per cent) in the sixteenth century, and a massive increase (57 per cent) in the twentieth century. Notice that during the nineteenth century life expectancy increased by only 12 per cent. On the other hand, these changes in life expectancy fail to confirm the pattern of real wage data over the same period compiled by Brown and Hopkins.[60]

The first wave of growth and its aftermath, 1000–1490

The simulated economic fluctuations in Figure 3.3, which are determined by a number of solid empirical benchmarks, suggest that there was a strong growth episode between 1000 and 1170 during which population grew at a compound rate of 0.7 per cent per annum and GDP per capita grew at 0.6 per cent per annum – double the rate for the entire six centuries. And there were probably shorter periods within these two centuries of upswing when the growth rate was even more rapid. This expansion and growth in real terms also corresponded to an increase in agricultural prices, which suggests that demand-side forces were driving the process of economic change in this period. Quite clearly this great wave of economic change was impressive even in comparison with the one we are currently experiencing.

It is widely accepted that expansion during the twelfth century ended around 1300 owing to the pressure of population on resources at a time when agrarian technology was largely static – a fact which is reflected in the stable wheat yields on Winchester estate manors.[61] Figure 3.3 confirms this interpretation. In fact these results suggest that growth may have ceased from the middle of the thirteenth century, at a time when population and real GDP continued to expand. The usual explanation is similar to that of the classical growth model, particularly the Malthusian version, in which the growth of population leads to the settlement of progressively less productive land, the emergence of diminishing returns on investment, and a steady decline in the productivity of labour. The effect of this, in the absence of any major new improvements in agricultural technology, is to reduce profits and wages, which in turn leads to a reduction in investment and population expansion until stagnation and even negative growth occurs. At first sight, therefore, the classical model appears far more relevant to the early fourteenth century than it ever was to the early nineteenth.[62] In any case, it would appear that a self-correcting downturn (exacerbated by the upsurge of accompanying domestic violence from 1307 to 1327) occurred before the impact of the Black Death in 1348 which, as a first approximation, can be treated as largely exogenous. After this dramatic decline, longrun stagnation set in owing to regular and frequent occurrences of pestilence and war (including the Hundred Years War from 1337 to 1453 and the Wars of the Roses from 1455 to 1485) which disrupted local economic activity and international trade. These events combined to cause this great wave of economic change to collapse.

Comparative static interpretations

My interpretation of this wave of economic change, both its powerful upsurge and its 'collapse', differs from the traditional wisdom. Scholars such as Ronald Lee, John Hatcher, Michael Postan, and Wilhelm Abel see this episode, as indeed they see the wider period 1250 to 1700, as being dominated by an inverse relationship between *long* swings in population and living standards. The reason for this rather curious view is that they take seriously the Brown–Hopkins real wage rate index. Accordingly they are forced to develop ingenious, but totally unrealistic, arguments to support untenable empirical relationships. Lee takes a particularly extreme position in this respect. He argues that economic growth is driven by exogenous forces that affect mortality. In this simple model, plague increases mortality, which in turn reduces population and leads to a backward shift of the supply of labour schedule (Figure 3.4(a)); as the demand for labour schedule is assumed to be fixed (on the heroic assumption that there are no longrun changes in technology, economies of scale, factor proportions, etc.), the real wage rate (w/p), which is treated as a proxy for per capita income, will rise. In Lee's words:

We conclude that the real wage and population size of pre-industrial England was regulated by an unchanging homeostatic system, in which exogenously varying mortality determined the equilibrium levels. We are left with the impression of great variation in the preindustrial period, but very little structural change prior to the eighteenth century.[63]

Hence longrun growth in this model is generated when population falls, and *negative* longrun growth occurs when population increases. This is a *very* strange growth model. I cannot think of any conceptual rationale or real-world support for such a model in a developed economy, apart from the fact that the author believes the Brown–Hopkins index of real wage rates. If the longrun relationship between population and per capita income is positive after 1700 (as it is shown to be in Figure 3.3), why should it be negative before 1700? A further point to note is that, contrary to Lee's claim above, there was in fact considerable structural change between 1086 and 1688, with urban population increasing from 8 to 20 per cent of the total. What was driving this structural change if it was not economic growth? Basically the view underlying this model is that human society has no internal dynamics and that it is like a straw blowing in the wind.

John Hatcher is clearly not comfortable with a model in which growth is only generated by exogenous forces. Yet he feels con-

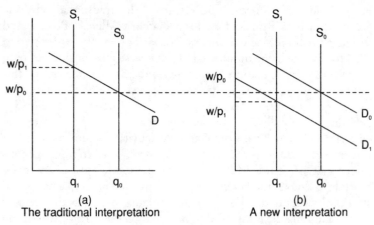

Figure 3.4 Demand and supply determinants of labour earnings following the Black Death, 1348

Source: See text

strained by the Brown–Hopkins index, and attempts to support the idea of a *longrun* inverse relationship between changes in population and living standards. Referring to the Brown–Hopkins index in conjunction with his population estimates Hatcher concludes:

> It can be seen at a glance that high population coincided with low living standards, and low population with high living standards, and that as population rose so living standards fell, and that as population fell so living standards rose.[64]

And these are not short-term relationships but rather relationships that persist for some 500 years. In attempting to explain one of these episodes, the Black Death, Hatcher argues:

> There are many good reasons why the reduction in population should have led to a rise in *per capita* output. It is now generally agreed that England, along with many parts of Europe, was suffering from some degree of overpopulation in the early fourteenth century, and that diminishing returns had long since begun to operate in many sectors of the economy. There is widespread evidence of the cultivation of poor soils at this time, of holdings far below the optimum size, and of an abundance of labour which inevitably produced chronic under- and un-employment. The subsequent reduction in population must have led to increased productivity by restoring a more efficient balance between labour, land and capital. The reduction in population must also have led to a sharp increase in *per capita* wealth and consumption. In simple terms, the survivors in-herited the property of those who had perished and, when presented with a sudden increase in wealth at a time of recurrent plague and considerable uncertainty, it is not surprising that they chose to spend on a greater scale than their predecessors. Demand was further stimulated by the increasing earnings of labourers and peasants; and there is also the possibility that these groups had a greater propensity to consume than land-lords and others who suffered a relative reduction in income.[65]

The reasons given by Hatcher fall into two categories. The first part of his argument, about an improvement in productivity resulting from the use of better quality land, is consistent with a move along the demand curve as represented in Figure 3.4(a). Basically it is a supply-side argument. The second part of Hatcher's explanation is far from clear. He claims that the sudden reduction in population

69

must have increased per capita wealth and consumption, which in turn would have increased aggregate demand, prices and, presumably through its impact on the marginal revenue–product curves for labour (which will move to the right), nominal wages. Unfortunately Hatcher has mixed together arguments about real and nominal wages in this paragraph.

Similar supply-side arguments, which are not always internally consistent, are advanced by scholars such as Abel and Postan. Abel, for example, argues that '[t]here were not enough men to till the soil; moreover, they demanded higher wages from the people who had been spared by the plague'; and again: 'As the arable shrank the supply of grain dwindled but, on the other hand, although there were also fewer consumers their purchasing power had increased. The many legacies they had inherited, together with the higher wages and prices, had given them a margin bigger than ever before.'[66] Postan also wrote about this period in a similar way: 'Increased demand for agricultural labour is difficult to reconcile with what we know of changes on demesnes'; and 'however effective may have been the additional demand for industrial labour, it was not as important a "real" factor behind the movement of wages as the changes in population'.[67] This is the familiar supply-side argument – the type of argument that is required to produce the increase in nominal and real wages shown in the Brown–Hopkins indexes.

The interpretation of Abel, Hatcher, and Postan concerning nominal markets either underplays or overlooks the effect of a massive reduction of population on aggregate demand in the English economy. In a closed economy, during those circumstances, the aggregate demand function will shift inwards at about the same rate as the aggregate supply function. But as the English economy in 1348 was not closed, it is highly likely that aggregate demand began falling at least a year before the aggregate supply function, because of the earlier impact of bubonic plague in Europe. The Black Death, which was first recorded in south-eastern Europe at the end of 1347, had reached Paris by June 1348, London by December 1348, and Edinburgh by the end of 1349.[68] This would have dramatically reduced export demand during 1347–48. After 1348 this export-led reduction in aggregate demand must have been accelerated by a sudden drop in consumption, investment, and government expenditures in England. The effect of this would have been twofold. First, the resulting fall in product prices – wheat prices did fall slightly in 1348 and more dramatically (37 per cent) in 1349 – would have caused the marginal revenue product curves for labour faced by producers to shift backwards, and for nominal wage rates to fall, at least during 1347–48. But, of course, this tells us nothing about real wages. Secondly, the demand schedule for land would also fall while the supply curve would remain fixed, thereby leading to a reduction in the price of land. The same is true of fixed capital, at least until the capital stock began to deteriorate, and also of movable goods. Hence there would be no major positive wealth effect as Hatcher and other historians have suggested.

A more likely outcome, based on the available evidence, is that presented in Figure 3.4(b). As in the first diagram, the labour supply schedule shifts to the left owing to the reduction of population by about 50 per cent in 1348. At the same time the labour demand schedule shifts even further to the left because of the impact of the Black Death on the nature of production and economic organization, with the result that the real wage falls. The underlying reasons for the leftward shift in the labour demand schedule are fourfold. First, the halving of the economy's size would have resulted in a backward shift along the longrun average cost curve, resulting in diseconomies of scale. These increased costs of production would have been signifi-cant, and would have persisted until expansion of the economy was underway again 150 years later. Secondly, the organization of the English economic system had to be adapted to a scale of operation that had existed 250 years before, and which none could remember. Inevitably organizational costs would have risen. Thirdly, the stock of physical capital would have declined dramatically through non-use and poor maintenance, particularly because of the high rates of depreciation on pre-industrial capital that was heavily labour-intensive. Meadowland, for example, depended upon the constant maintenance of irrigation and drainage channels; watermills un-attended quickly fell into disrepair;[69] and livestock strayed or were killed by predators when left unattended. Also much human capital would have been lost. Finally, there may even have been a degree of technological regress, at least in the first few decades after the onslaught of the Black Death, because of the sudden change in scale and factor endowments (and hence relative factor prices). The appropriate form of technology would have been similar to that which existed in the early twelfth century. These arguments are not just relevant to the period after the Black Death, they are applicable in reverse to the earlier and later periods of expansion and growth.

Since this argument was first developed in my book *Economics without Time*, further and more appropriate real wage rate data (concerning rural activities) have come to light. Larry Poos's work on the nominal wages and prices contained in the manorial records of Essex show that real wages declined by about 24 per cent immediately after the Black Death, and this lower level was maintained until the late fifteenth century.[70] Also, tax data show that no new taxes were imposed immediately after the Black Death, that there was an attempt to shift the tax burden to felons, that from the 1370s attempts were made to reduce the burden on land by experiments with a Parish Tax and Poll Taxes, that during the early 1400s attempts were made to tax aliens, and that throughout the fifteenth century there were considerable taxation abatements and exemptions.[71]

Dynamic interpretations

The second theoretical argument against the conventional hypothesis is of a dynamic nature. It is just not plausible to argue that a country experiencing a long and savage downswing in population will experience a sustained increase in real per capita income – sustained, according to Brown and Hopkins, for over a century. Those who subscribe to an argument of this nature appear not to have given any consideration to the dynamics of such an economy. There are a number of fundamental questions that need to be asked. What is the driving force in such a growth process? In particular, what could possibly generate such a sustained increase in living standards? Obviously it is not the incentive effect of population expansion, because population is declining, at first savagely, and then steadily for at least a century. It is hardly likely to be capital accumulation, because a decline in population of this magnitude, as argued above, would have resulted in a steady decline in capital stock. The available evidence reinforces this conclusion.[72] Could it, however, have resulted from a dramatic increase in productive efficiency? Certainly it is not a result of economies of scale as the size of the economy was halved; and technological advance, after the initial technological regress, does not appear to have been significant as Hatcher, among others, refers to 'relatively static technology' during this period.[73] In any case owing to the massive reduction in population there was little incentive – and owing to disinvestment there were limited opportunities – for the introduction of embodied technology. Even positive institutional change involving a reduction of transactions costs would have been unlikely in this period – a period when the pressure to adapt to population increase had been dramatically reduced. The upshot of this argument, therefore, is that there is no obvious candidate for a long-term expansion of living standards during this period of population decline. It is more likely that the expansion of real wage rates detected by Brown and Hopkins – with the possible exception of the last few decades of the fourteenth century[74] – is a statistical illusion.[75]

The second and third waves of growth

The second and shortest wave of growth during the past millennium began at the end of the fifteenth century and proceeded at a more rapid pace – approximately 1.3 per cent per annum for a century – than did growth during the first episode; so rapid that it grew 2.5 times faster than population (at 0.5 per cent per annum) over the same period (see Figure 3.3). A growth rate of this magnitude can compare favourably with the Industrial Revolution or, indeed, with anything achieved in England during the nineteenth and twentieth centuries for a comparable period of time. Actually, growth during the first half of the period appears to have been about double that of the second half. And once again this wave of growth was accompanied by an upsurge in agricultural prices, implicating demand-side forces. This episode of economic growth probably owed more to the re-establishment of political order, to organizational changes (and resulting reductions in transactions costs), to the growth of towns, and to the rapid expansion of overseas trade (extending both the natural resource base and the scope for specialization), than to technological change.[76]

Indeed, in terms of its duration and rate of change, this wave of growth appears to have been very much conditioned by the previous one and one-half centuries of demographic and military disruption. Without this drawn-out exogenous shock, the growth of GDP per capita to 1620 probably would have extended over a longer period of time, perhaps 200 to 300 years, and would have taken place at a correspondingly slower rate. By the early seventeenth century, however, this amazing wave of growth began to break at a population level approximately equivalent to that in 1300 – about 5.5 million – but at a per capita income level almost three times higher. Following a period of impressive expansion and growth, continued population pressure on natural resources during a period of limited technological change and declining trade (from the late 1610s)[77] appears to have brought economic expansion temporarily to an end. Unlike the downturn after 1300, this period of stagnation was temporary because it did not coincide with an exogenous shock of the proportions of the Black Death. Instead it was a period in which economic agents were free to respond to the market forces generated by population pressure on natural resources. The response was the application of new techniques of production to agriculture and industry that came to be known as the Industrial Revolution. It would appear that without a major change in agricultural and industrial technology and a transformation of transport and communications, the English population would not exceed 6.0 million. This implies that the economic contribution of the Industrial Revolution should be seen not in terms of the rate of economic change – it was less impressive than that of both the sixteenth century and the tenth and eleventh centuries – but in terms of making it possible to break the nexus between population and natural resources that had harried the Middle Ages.

The third and final phase of expansion and growth, also accompanied by rising prices, began in the mid-eighteenth century – with antecedents stretching back into the seventeenth century – quickly gathering momentum until, by 1800, it was proceeding at a relatively rapid, but not a historically abnormal, rate. This rate of growth was maintained until the middle of the nineteenth century, after which it began to slow down gradually, and then, after the First World War, quite suddenly. There was an impressive, but brief, acceleration in the 1950s and 1960s, with slower growth thereafter. The interesting point is that during the third phase of expansion, population was able to escape from its low level of 5.5 million in 1700 to reach 50.7 million in 1990 because of the major changes that occurred in technology, infrastructure, and economic organization from the mid-eighteenth century.[78] It is possible that in the very near future we will be facing a natural resources constraint as serious as that which prevailed throughout the later Middle Ages. If so it may take a change in technology and social organization as major and as unpredictable as that of the Industrial Revolution to prevent prolonged stagnation and instability.

WHAT ARE THE IMPLICATIONS OF A FORWARD-LOOKING PERSPECTIVE?

By placing the Industrial Revolution within the context of economic change during the last millennium we do gain a different perspective on this great event in human history. In the first place, it is suggested in this chapter that rapid and sustained rates of economic growth are not a modern invention. In terms of rates of economic growth, the Industrial Revolution was not a radical departure from what had been experienced in the periods 1000 to 1300 and, particularly, the sixteenth century. It has also been argued that growth over the last millennium has been a systematic process – a process of continuous transformation – rather than a series of random events. And this systematic growth process has proceeded via a succession of 'great waves' of economic change, of up to 300 years in duration.

This wave-like growth process, which has involved a *positive* relationship between population and real GDP per capita, is driven by fundamental endogenous economic forces rather than by exogenously determined demographic forces. And a major actor in this process is economic man. But this endogenous process is subject to exogenous shocks in the form of pestilence and war, both civil and from foreign aggression. This view is to be contrasted with those that characterize longrun growth as being exogenously determined by an impact upon mortality and proceeding via inverse longrun swings in population and real GDP per capita. Growth, therefore, should be viewed not as a result of random events, but rather as a natural internally generated outcome of competitive societies.

This continuous process of economic transformation was achieved in different ways in different periods. Longrun growth is not just a function of industrialization. For example, during the period 1000 to 1300, while there was a slow improvement in the technological foundations of agriculture, urban activities, and transport, the major part of this growth was due to the emergence of factor markets (particularly for labour and capital), and the widening of commodity markets, all of which reduced transactions costs.[79] Indeed the great transformation from feudalism to mercantile capitalism should be thought of as being caused by the emergence of factor markets. Similarly, during the period from the 1490s to the 1620s, changes in the organizational nature of the economy were an important source of growth, although the development of overseas markets (with its impact upon specialization) and higher levels of the capital/labour ratio were becoming increasingly important. And the period between these two vigorous upswings – 1350 to 1490 – was not static. Fundamental economic forces were changing the organizational structure of medieval society, even if the outcome in terms of changes in population and GDP per capita were constrained by the vicelike grip of pestilence and war. Hence, the uniqueness of the Industrial Revolution is not in terms of the speed of economic change but in the role played by technological change and industrialization in this process, together with the implications for population expansion of the breakdown in the medieval nexus between population and natural resources.

Finally, by taking a very longrun perspective, we can see that the rate of modern growth, which began with the Industrial Revolution, is not accelerating as suggested by the 'new' growth theorists. Indeed, when one allows for the exceptional circumstances of the 1950s and 1960s – in part a reaction to the steely grip of depression and war in the 1930s and 1940s (and in this sense similar to the exceptional nature of the sixteenth century) – it is clear that modern growth rates are not accelerating. There are, and have always been, limits to growth, and these limits have been approached in the past. There is nothing 'new' in this.

APPENDIX

Table 3.7 Estimated population, income, and prices, England, 1086–1700
(selected years)

Year	Population (millions)	Real GDP in 1688 prices (£m)	Real GDP per capita in 1688 prices (£)	Wheat prices shillings per quarter (11 year moving average)
1086	1.53	2.63	1.72	–
1115	1.91	3.85	2.02	–
1127	2.10	4.55	2.17	–
1138	2.27	5.40	2.38	–
1150	2.50	6.00	2.40	–
1160	2.67	7.00	2.62	–
1170	2.87	7.80	2.72	–
1180	3.08	8.80	2.86	–
1190	3.30	9.70	2.94	–
1203	3.59	11.00	3.06	–
1210	3.77	11.60	3.08	–
1220	4.00	13.00	3.25	–
1232	4.35	14.00	3.22	–
1250	4.90	16.20	3.31	–
1260	5.15	16.80	3.26	–
1270	5.42	17.70	3.27	5.29
1280	5.62	18.50	3.29	5.59
1300	5.75	19.00	3.30	5.51
1310	5.75	18.50	3.22	5.96
1320	5.70	17.70	3.11	8.98
1330	5.62	16.00	2.85	5.54
1340	5.44	15.00	2.76	4.31
1347	5.25	13.50	2.57	5.68
1350	5.15	12.00	2.33	5.96
1360	4.30	9.00	2.09	6.66
1370	3.38	6.90	2.04	7.73
1377	2.75	6.00	2.18	6.04
1380	2.68	5.70	2.13	5.54
1390	2.55	5.30	2.08	4.72
1400	2.48	5.00	2.02	5.75
1410	2.40	4.90	2.04	4.95
1420	2.35	5.00	2.13	5.35
1430	2.30	4.90	2.13	5.50
1440	2.27	4.80	2.12	6.14
1450	2.25	4.85	2.16	5.23
1470	2.28	4.90	2.15	5.08
1480	2.30	5.00	2.17	6.34
1490	2.32	5.25	2.26	4.98
1500	2.36	6.10	2.58	5.64
1510	2.39	7.80	3.26	5.46

Table 3.7 continued

Year	Population (millions)	Real GDP in 1688 prices (£m)	Real GDP per capita in 1688 prices (£)	Wheat prices shilling per quarter (11 year moving average)
1520	2.43	9.00	3.70	6.32
1525	2.50	10.70	4.28	8.19
1530	2.55	11.00	4.31	8.47
1540	2.70	13.50	5.00	8.40
1546	2.85	14.00	4.91	10.36
1550	2.97	15.50	5.22	12.96
1560	2.96	20.00	6.75	16.24
1570	3.26	22.80	7.00	13.89
1580	3.57	27.00	7.57	18.35
1590	3.90	31.00	7.96	25.00
1600	4.07	37.00	9.10	34.33
1610	4.39	40.00	9.11	35.05
1620	4.64	42.00	9.06	36.73
1630	4.88	45.50	9.32	40.42
1640	5.06	48.00	9.50	40.86
1648	5.23	49.00	9.38	49.72
1660	5.13	49.50	9.65	45.66
1670	5.02	49.00	9.76	38.43
1680	4.99	48.50	9.72	41.08
1690	4.92	48.64	9.89	35.35
1700	5.03	51.29	10.20	38.23

Source: Data underlying Figure 3.3. See note 58 for estimation procedure

Notes: The wheat price series (from Rogers, *Agriculture and Prices*, and Farmer, 'Angevin England') presented here was *not* used for deflation purposes.

The population series is based upon Snooks, *Economics without Time*, Hatcher, *Plague, Population* before 1540, and Wrigley and Schofield, *Population* after 1540. The population estimate here for the end of the period differs slightly from that based upon Gregory King used in Table 3.2 (for the same reason the estimate of real GDP also differs slightly – but not real GDP per capita).

4

WHAT WAS THE RATE OF ECONOMIC GROWTH DURING THE INDUSTRIAL REVOLUTION?

R. V. Jackson

What *was* the rate of economic growth in Britain during the Industrial Revolution? In the 1960s, Deane and Cole's enquiry into the surviving statistical evidence appeared to have established a broad answer to this question.[1] A new phase of rapid growth was seen as having begun in the 1780s and the apparent contrast with the past was so marked that Deane and Cole regarded the revolutionary character of the change as being beyond doubt.[2] This view of the Industrial Revolution, however, has now fallen from favour and the new orthodoxy is that growth remained slow and uncertain until the 1820s. The rise of the new orthodoxy is due mainly to the work of Harley and Crafts.[3] The present chapter concentrates on Crafts's revisions of Deane and Cole's estimates of the growth of national product between 1780 and 1831.

Deane and Cole readily acknowledged that their growth estimates for this period were built on slight foundations and that much of their processing of the statistical raw material was highly subjective.[4] They envisaged a programme of future research which would place the estimates on a sounder footing and which might well modify their results. Some of this has come to pass, for Deane and Cole's results have indeed been overturned. The new orthodoxy, however, is based less upon new evidence about the course of production than upon different ways of interpreting the very evidence to which Deane and Cole themselves appealed. These differences in interpretation, more-over, reflect different assumptions about the workings of the economy rather than a deeper knowledge of what was happening in Britain during the Industrial Revolution: Crafts' new estimates effectively presuppose that growth after 1780 was slower than Deane and Cole had thought.

This is one instance of a more general problem facing historians who seek to measure the rate of economic growth in the longrun past. As the statistical raw materials are meagre and relate only indirectly to the concept of real product, the construction of indicators of economic growth inevitably depends upon assumptions about the structure of economic relationships during the period under investigation. An interpretation of the economy is thus incorporated into the growth indicators themselves. Indeed, the indicators developed in this way are valuable precisely because they make explicit some of the quantitative implications of a particular line of reasoning about the pattern of economic change. And, so long as their dependence on a particular view of the economy is kept in mind, these growth indicators may also be a valuable aid to further analysis. The statistical raw material, however, is usually open to a variety of interpretations. In the case of Britain during the Industrial Revolution, small differences in initial assumptions can produce very different results. This sensitivity of the growth estimates to initial assumptions does not establish that Crafts and his fellow revisionists are mistaken in their belief that growth was slow, for the growth rates which they have calculated are broadly consistent with the evidence when it is viewed in a particular way. The estimates themselves, however, do not provide independent support for the revisionist position. They are essentially an illustration of the orders of magnitude that are implicit in the revisionist view of the economy during this period, not a demonstration that growth was indeed slow. Within wide limits, the rate of economic growth during the Industrial Revolution remains an open question.

OLD AND NEW VIEWS OF THE RATE OF ECONOMIC GROWTH

An influential early contribution to the revisionists' case came from Harley who argued that the rate of industrial growth before 1815 had been exaggerated by earlier writers.[5] Harley's main attack was upon the Hoffmann index of industrial production, but his work also cut much of the ground from under Deane and Cole.[6] Though the Hoffmann index had long been thought to be unreliable for the eighteenth century, Harley's clinical dissection of the index and his new calculations showing slower industrial growth were decisive steps in the emergence of the revisionist view. In essence, Harley appeared to have demonstrated that at the very heart of the Industrial Revolution, in the industrial sector itself, growth had been far slower than either Hoffmann or Deane and Cole had imagined.

The revised interpretation implicit in Harley's work on industrial growth was generalized and articulated in detail by Crafts. On the basis of his own estimates of national product, Crafts argued that growth was 'considerably slower between 1780 and 1821–30 than was believed by Deane and Cole' and that 'the acceleration of growth was a more gradual process than metaphors such as "take-off" imply'.[7] Crafts has since reduced his estimate of the rate of growth after 1801 still further,[8] and Table 4.1 compares his most recent estimates with those of Deane and Cole. On Crafts's reckoning, Deane and Cole overestimated the annual growth of real national product by 0.5 percentage points between 1780 and 1801, by 0.9 percentage points between 1801 and 1831, and by 0.7 percentage points over the whole period 1780 to 1831. The effect of these differences in annual growth rates is very large when cumulated over several decades. Deane and Cole's estimates imply that national product was 3.4 times as large in 1831 as it had been in 1780, while Crafts' estimates imply growth to only 2.4 times the 1780 level. More striking still is the contrast between the 80 per cent increase in product per head between 1780 and 1831 that is implicit in Deane and Cole's estimates and the rise of only 25 per cent shown by Crafts's estimates.

Table 4.1 Growth of real national product, 1700–1831 (per cent per year)

Period	Deane and Cole		Crafts	
	National product	National product per head	National product	National product per head
1700–1780	0.6	0.2	0.7	0.2
1780–1801	1.9	0.9	1.4	0.4
1801–1831	2.8	1.3	1.9	0.5
1780–1831	2.4	1.2	1.7	0.4

Sources: Deane and Cole, *British Economic Growth*, pp. 6, 8, 78–80, 282; Crafts, *British Economic Growth*, p. 45, as amended in Crafts and Harley, 'Output growth', p. 715. The Deane and Cole figures for the eighteenth century are the average of the annual growth rates of real output shown by their estimates using a 1700 and an 1800 base

THE EIGHTEENTH CENTURY

What is the basis of the new view of the rate of growth? Consider first the period up to 1801. Crafts's revisions of the estimated growth rate in this period do not depend on new evidence brought to light by extensive new research. Rather, the evidence available to Deane and Cole has been interpreted differently. Much of the difference in interpretation has arisen directly from the assumptions which Crafts has made about the ways in which various parts of the economy were related to each other, and this has implications for the uses to which the growth estimates can be put.

As it is not possible to build a set of national income accounts to show the growth of real product in the eighteenth century, reliance on indirect estimation procedures is unavoidable. Ostensibly, Deane and Cole calculated an index of total real output as the weighted average of output growth in five sectors of the economy. Because they relied heavily on proxies to indicate sectoral growth, however, their index is really the weighted average of these proxy indicators. Deane and Cole used population growth to indicate the growth of output in agriculture and in rent and services.[9] The volume of foreign trade was used as a proxy for the growth of the export industries and net real government expenditure out of the exchequer was taken as a proxy for government output. The output of home industries was calculated more directly as the weighted average of the excise series for beer, leather, candles, and soap.

Deane and Cole's basic estimate of total real output in both 1780 and 1800 can be represented as being approximately

$$Y = 0.63P + 0.18F + 0.12H + 0.07G \tag{1}$$

where each variable is an index number based on 1700, P is population, F is domestic exports plus imports, H is the output of home industry, and G is net government expenditure.

Crafts's procedure for this period can also be reduced to a simple formula. He identified five sectors: agriculture, industry, commerce, rent and services, and government. Population growth was taken as a proxy for the growth in the demand for agricultural products which would have taken place had relative prices and real income per head remained the same throughout the eighteenth century. In estimating the growth of agricultural output, Crafts made an allowance for changes in prices and income on the assumption that the price and income elasticities of demand for agricultural products were −0.8 and

0.7 respectively. He estimated industrial growth on the basis of output indicators for thirteen industries. While this treatment of industry was a movement towards the use of more direct estimation methods for the eighteenth century, Crafts also took a step back in the direction of proxy variables by assuming that the commercial sector grew at the same rate as the economy as a whole. Crafts followed Deane and Cole in using government expenditure as a measure of government output and population as a proxy for rent and services.

This procedure can be summarized as a set of equations:

$$Y = aA + iI + cC + sS + gG \tag{2}$$
$$A = P + eR + n(Y-P) \tag{3}$$
$$I = I \tag{4}$$
$$C = Y \tag{5}$$
$$S = P \tag{6}$$
$$G = G \tag{7}$$

where upper-case letters are annual percentage rates of growth, Y is national product, A is agriculture, I is industry, C is commerce, S is rent and services, G is government, P is population, and R is the relative price of agricultural products. The lower-case letters in equation 2 are weights which sum to one, and e and n in equation 3 are the price and income elasticities of demand for agricultural products. Substitution of equations 3 to 7 into equation 2 and solving for Y gives

$$Y = [(a-an+s)P + aeR + iI + gG]/(1-an-c) \tag{8}$$

With the sectoral weights Crafts used for the period 1780–1801, equation 8 becomes

$$Y = 0.41P - 0.30R + 0.48I + 0.11G \tag{9}$$

A comparison of equations (1) and (9) shows that Crafts dropped foreign trade as a proxy variable, made an adjustment to allow for changes in the price of agricultural products, expanded the index of home industry to refer to the whole of the industrial sector, retained government expenditure as an indicator of government output, and used different weights to combine these various elements into an aggregate index of growth.

Crafts drew upon research that had not been available to Deane and Cole in estimating some of the terms in equation (9). This new research, however, was not the source of the lower growth rates he found for the period 1780 to 1801. The rate of population growth he used is virtually identical to that used by Deane and Cole.[10] The increase in the relative price of agricultural products was slower in his reckoning than in Deane and Cole's, so that his estimate of the growth in national product would have been even lower had he used their figures for agricultural prices.[11] On the basis of Lindert and Williamson's social tables, Crafts gave more weight to industry and less to agriculture than Deane and Cole had done.[12] Again, this would have raised his estimate of the aggregate growth rate. The social tables, however, also provided Crafts with a justification for treating commerce in a way which lowered the measured growth of this sector relative to the growth he would have found had he followed Deane and Cole.[13] New research formed the basis of his estimates of coal, iron, and building output, but in each case growth was either faster than or similar to that implied by earlier estimates.[14] For the rest of the industrial sector, Crafts's calculations depended very largely upon detailed work done by Deane and Cole themselves or upon elementary calculations using the excise and trade statistics collected by Mitchell and Deane.[15] Clearly, Deane and Cole could have used this material to extend their index of home industry to cover the rest of the industrial sector, but they chose instead to use the growth of foreign trade as a proxy.

Inevitably, Crafts's estimates of the terms in equation (9) are subject to error, for the data upon which they are based are incomplete, often unreliable, and generally refer only indirectly to the variable in question. The population figures are for England rather than for Great Britain as Crafts would have preferred.[16] Estimates of the relative price of agricultural products vary widely and are unreliable because of poor data for industrial products and services.[17] Nor is the change in the relative price of agricultural products a fully independent piece of information in equation (9), for Crafts derived his estimate of the change in relative prices in a way which aimed to reconcile the incomplete price data with the sectoral growth rates he had already identified.[18] Estimates of industrial growth in the eighteenth century depend as much on the procedures applied to the available statistical evidence as they do on the evidence itself: the growth rates shown by two estimates which are based on nearly identical statistical material differ by 1.5 percentage points a year in the period 1780 to 1801 as a result of simple differences in procedure.[19] The industrial growth estimates take no account of any increase which may have occurred in output per unit of materials input, because each estimate has been derived from data on the growth of output or of inputs of raw materials in the various industries. And, while the series for government expenditure is an accurate record of the amounts passing through the exchequer, it is no guide to movements in government expenditure of the kind relevant to the calculation of national product, because it excludes most of the expenditure on goods and services that arose out of the administration of the civil establishment and includes large transfer payments and payments to foreigners.[20]

More fundamental, however, is that in using the variables in equation (9) to estimate the growth of national product Crafts has in effect assumed that a particular structure of economic relationships prevailed. An interpretation of the economic experience of the period is thus built into the estimating process and is embodied in the estimates at both the aggregate and the sectoral level. Crafts's estimates differ from Deane and Cole's because he has made different assumptions about the form of these economic relationships and because he has attached a different meaning to indicators which do not bear directly on the measurement of national product. To the extent that they are the arithmetical consequence of his view of the economy, Crafts's growth estimates provide no independent check of the validity of his interpretation. The usefulness of the estimates in the analysis of economic change is also limited because implicit answers to key questions are already embedded in the estimating procedure.

These points can be illustrated by reference to the role given to population in the estimates. In assuming that the consumption of services and agricultural products grew at the same rate as population, Deane and Cole assumed that income and prices had no effect on the consumption of these products. Crafts treated services in the same way but his procedure for agriculture was based on the assumption that consumption varied directly with income per head and inversely with the price of agricultural products. This is consistent with conventional economic theory and this consistency makes Crafts's estimates seem more reasonable than Deane and Cole's. Crafts's treatment of agriculture, however, also means that his estimates are not independent of his views of the way in which the economy operated. Thus agricultural consumption is assumed to have responded to prices and to average real income but not to changes in taste, income distribution, social and economic organization, or industrial structure (which is relevant because agriculture produced industrial raw materials as well as consumption goods).[21]

Similarly, equation (9) presupposes that a particular relationship existed between population and aggregate real product, with an increase in population being associated with an increase in product but a fall in product per head. Had Crafts used figures for British population, which grew more slowly than the English population in the late eighteenth century, he would have found aggregate growth to be slower and growth per head to have been faster. Such a result, of course, is consistent with the predictions of static theory and this view may well be accurate for this period. It is none the less unfortunate to have to rely upon growth estimates which embody this or any other assumption about the economic consequences of population growth.

The difficulties which arise from this use of population in the estimating process are exemplified by Crafts's own discussion of the sources of economic growth in the eighteenth century.[22] As we have seen, Crafts estimated the growth in national product during 1780 to 1801 by

$$Y = 0.41P + Z \tag{10}$$

where Z is the sum of the terms besides population in equation (9). For the period 1700 to 1780 Crafts estimated growth by

$$Y = 0.54P + Z \tag{11}$$

with the difference in the weight given to population growth being due to the different sectoral weights he used in this period. Having estimated growth in this way, Crafts went on to analyse the extent to which growth could be explained by the growth of inputs. Aggregate growth was decomposed into

$$Y = 0.50L + 0.35K + 0.15T + r \tag{12}$$

with L, K, and T being the annual rates of growth of inputs of labour, capital, and land, and r being that part of the growth of total product which was not attributable to the increase in factor inputs. Crafts measured the growth of labour inputs by the growth rate of the population aged 15 to 59 which was approximately equal to the growth rate of total population. Had he measured L by P his results would not have been materially affected. The circularity of the analysis is clear if P is substituted for L in equation 12 and if this is compared with equations (10) and (11).

Crafts's growth estimates thus rest on particular assumptions about the structure and functioning of the economy. The estimates, moreover, are sensitive to the precise form which these assumptions about economic relationships happen to take. Suppose, for example, that we stay within the framework of the interpretation which is implicit in Crafts's calculations but allow a small amount of slippage in the estimating procedure. The independent elements in the procedure are the estimates of population, industrial production, government expenditure, and the relative price of agricultural products.[23] The relationships which allow these elements to be translated into estimates of the rate of growth of national product are the income and price elasticities of demand for agricultural products, the assumption that commerce grew at the same rate as total product, and the assumption that services grew at the same rate as population. To test the sensitivity of the results to small changes in these variables and in the assumptions used, let the annual growth rate in industry and government and the trend in agricultural prices vary by a small amount around the figures used by Crafts. Also let the growth in commerce differ from the growth of national product and let the growth in rent and services output differ from population growth by the same amount.[24] If the envisaged variation is plus or minus v percentage points, the estimate of the rate of growth of national product varies by plus or minus

$$v(a\,|e|+i+c+s+g)/(1-an-c)$$

If v is 0.1 percentage points, the estimate of the annual growth rate of national product varies by up to 0.14 percentage points in either direction in the period 1780 to 1801, giving aggregate growth of 1.24 to 1.52 per cent a year. For earlier periods, Crafts gave different weights to agriculture and industry, which means that for these periods a v of 0.1 percentage points involves a variation in the growth rate of national product of plus or minus 0.16 percentage points. An allowance for error of 0.1 percentage points is very small considering the likely accuracy of the component series but it is sufficient to make the growth estimates virtually useless for important analytical purposes, as Table 4.2 shows. On these assumptions, the growth of real product per head may have slowed somewhat after 1780 or it may have accelerated, perhaps by a little and perhaps by a lot. Over the century as a whole, real product per head may have risen by only 10 per cent or by as much as 50 per cent or by something in between. Very different patterns of economic growth are thus consistent with the underlying data even if we are content to

Table 4.2 Growth rates of real national product consistent with v = 0.1 percentage points, 1700–1801 (per cent per year)

	1700–1780		1780–1801	
	Minimum	*Maximum*	*Minimum*	*Maximum*
National product	0.52	0.84	1.24	1.52
Product per head	0.06	0.38	0.27	0.55

Source: See text.

remain within the spirit of the estimating procedure on which the new view of the matter rests.

THE EARLY NINETEENTH CENTURY

Deane and Cole used more direct methods for the period 1801 to 1831 than for the eighteenth century. They began by calculating the value of gross national product in current prices at ten-year intervals using the income approach. Labour income in most of the private sector was estimated by multiplying numbers employed in various activities by average money wage rates, and labour income in the public sector was derived directly from government accounts. Estimates of non-labour income were based on tax assessments supplemented by data on housing stock and average rents. Notional allocations were made for some professional incomes and for incomes from self-employment. Though gaps in the data had frequently to be filled arbitrarily, Deane and Cole were able to avoid strong assumptions about how various parts of the economy were related to each other. The allocation of the total among the various sectors depended heavily on guesswork, however, and their estimates of nominal income for any particular sector are less secure than their estimate for the economy as a whole.

Deane and Cole deflated their estimates sector by sector using the Rousseaux price indexes averaged over periods of nine years. The Rousseaux index for agricultural products was used for the agricultural group of industries, the index for industrial products was used for manufacturing, mining, and building, and the unweighted average of the indexes for agricultural and industrial products was used for the rest of the economy. The deflated estimates for each sector were then added together to arrive at gross national product in constant prices in each benchmark year. Deficiencies in the Rousseaux price indexes mean that Deane and Cole's estimates of real national product are more suspect than their estimates in current prices.[25] Indeed, the index of industrial prices (and hence the composite price index for services) is so poor that Crafts felt unable to follow Deane and Cole's basic procedure for the industrial and service sectors. Instead, he fell back upon methods akin to those he had used for the eighteenth century. Growth indexes were developed for each sector and these sectoral indexes were combined into an index of overall growth using weights based on Deane and Cole's estimate of the share of each sector in national product in 1821.

While Deane and Cole published summary estimates of total real product for the period 1801 to 1831,[26] they did not report separate real product figures for the various sectors. A sector by sector comparison with Crafts thus requires a reconstruction of their disaggregated estimates. In his discussion of Deane and Cole, Crafts made extensive use of the reconstructed figures shown in the first column of Table 4.3. These figures, however, are inconsistent with Deane and Cole's limited reporting of their results, perhaps because the price instability of this period makes the deflated estimates sensitive to the smoothing procedure used. The reconstruction in the second column of the table uses Deane and Cole's data, follows their deflation procedures so far as is possible, and is consistent with the aggregate figures they report for real product.[27]

Table 4.3 Growth of real national product, 1801–31 (per cent per year)

Sector	Reconstruction of Deane and Cole		Crafts
	Crafts	Jackson	
Agriculture, forestry, fishing	1.64	1.36	1.18
Manufactures, mining, building	4.44	4.23	2.78
Trade and transport	3.02	2.65	2.13
Domestic and personal services	3.12	2.75	1.37
Housing	3.75	3.39	1.53
Government, professional, and all other	1.97	1.92	1.37
National product	3.06	2.76	1.90

Source: See text

89

Crafts accepted Deane and Cole's estimates of agricultural income in current prices in 1801 and 1831 and judged their deflation procedure for agriculture to be 'much less problematic' than their use of the Rousseaux price indexes for other sectors.[28] He chose, none the less, to deflate agricultural income using O'Brien's index of agricultural prices to 1820 extended to 1831 on the basis of price data in Mitchell and Deane and in Beveridge.[29] The new deflator reduced the rate of growth of real agricultural output by 0.18 percentage points to 1.18 per cent a year, which Crafts regarded as being 'essentially consistent' with Deane and Cole.[30] One source of concern, however, was that the application of the demand approach which he had used for the eighteenth century suggested agricultural growth of 1.88 per cent a year between 1801 and 1831. Crafts thought the discrepancy might be due partly to errors in Deane and Cole's figure for agricultural income in 1831 and partly to changes in income distribution which might have reduced the price elasticity of demand for agricultural products in this period. This is a reminder of the dangers inherent in the use of indirect methods to estimate agricultural output.[31]

Crafts abandoned Deane and Cole's basic approach when he came to measure the growth of industry and services. His industrial growth estimates were a continuation of those he had developed for the eighteenth century and the comments made in the previous section also apply here. Proxies were used for the services sector. The growth in house rents was estimated by the growth in Feinstein's estimates of the real housing stock.[32] Real transport output was taken as the weighted average of the growth in real output on the Leeds–Liverpool canal and the growth in stage carriage travel.[33] Growth in real output in government, professional, and miscellaneous services was estimated using Williamson's work on wages and occupational structure in conjunction with employment figures from Deane and Cole.[34] The growth in employment was used as a proxy for output growth in the remainder of the services sector. Numbers employed in domestic and personal service were taken directly from Deane and Cole.[35] Employment in trade, however, had to be estimated indirectly because Deane and Cole gave only a combined figure for trade and transport before 1841.

Table 4.4 shows the extent to which the revisions to the growth estimates for each sector contributed to the slower growth of national product in Crafts's estimates compared with Deane and Cole's. These contributions have been derived by subtracting the third

Table 4.4 Sources of slower growth in Crafts's estimates of national product compared with Deane and Cole, 1801–31

Sector	Percentage points of annual growth
Agriculture, forestry, fishing	0.05
Manufactures, mining, building	0.46
Trade and transport	0.08
Domestic and personal services	0.08
Housing	0.11
Government, professional, and all other	0.08
National product	0.86

Source: See text

column from the second column in Table 4.3 and multiplying by the weights which Crafts gave to each sector in his calculations. About half the difference between the old and the new estimates of the rate of economic growth is due to revisions to the rate of industrial growth and most of the remainder is due to revisions to the growth of services.

Agriculture, housing, and the government and professional sector are the only areas of the economy for which Crafts's results depended to any extent on research undertaken after the publication of Deane and Cole's estimates. In government and the professions, moreover, this new research suggested that labour productivity grew somewhat faster than Deane and Cole's real product and employment estimates had implied.[36] Crafts's downward revisions to the rate of growth in agriculture and housing drew on the work of O'Brien and Feinstein. Since Crafts first wrote, however, Feinstein has produced new estimates which show somewhat faster growth in the real housing stock over this period and these new housing estimates have not been incorporated into Crafts's latest revisions.[37]

New research producing new information about the economy made no further significant contribution to Crafts' calculations. This is so even in trade and transport, where Crafts appealed explicitly to Hawke's work to derive a figure for the growth of transport output. As we have seen, Crafts took a weighted average of growth in trade and growth in transport as an indicator of growth in trade and transport combined, and he took growth in employment in trade as a proxy for growth in trade output. Growth in employment in trade, however, was derived partly from his estimate of the growth in real transport output. Crafts worked with Deane and Cole's figures for employment in trade and transport combined in 1801 and 1831. On the basis of their disaggregated employment figures for 1841, he gave transport a 75 per cent share of employment in trade and transport in 1831. He then assumed that employment in transport grew at an annual rate which was 0.4 percentage points below the growth in transport output. This gave him an estimate of numbers employed in transport in 1801 and allowed him to calculate employment in trade in that year as a residual. On these procedures, his estimate of the growth in trade employment (and hence output) will vary inversely with his estimate of the growth in transport output. Because of this inversity, Crafts's estimate of output growth in trade and transport combined is insensitive to the figure he used for transport growth.[38]

New evidence thus had little role to play in Crafts's revisions of Deane and Cole's estimates for this period. As in the eighteenth century, revisions of the rate of growth of real national product arose from looking at old evidence in a new way. In a sense, everything else depended upon Crafts's rejection of the Rousseaux indexes as deflators for industry and services, because this forced him to devise a set of alternative procedures for these sectors. This said, however, he then relied partly on assumptions which had no clear evidential basis and partly on a more direct reworking of the available evidence.

Assumptions about productivity change in industry and services played a key role. Crafts estimated the rate of industrial growth in both the eighteenth and early nineteenth centuries using material with which Deane and Cole were familiar but which they chose not to use. His calculations were of necessity based on the growth of materials input in some industries and on the growth of output in others, rather than upon indicators of the growth of real product. Any growth in productivity which took the form of economizing on materials inputs and any industrial growth which arose out of a more elaborate transformation of materials thus had no impact on his index. Crafts himself once argued that the Hoffmann index, which exploited similar statistical material, was for this reason a lower-bound estimate of industrial growth.[39] The application of similar reasoning to his own estimate of industrial growth would suggest that it should also be treated as a lower bound even though it is an unbiased estimate of the average rate of growth of the input and output indicators on which it is based.[40] At present there is no way in which we can avoid making an arbitrary assumption about the rate of growth of industrial output per unit of materials input. In his early paper, Crafts thought that Hoffmann's estimate of the annual rate of industrial growth might need to be raised by as much as half a percentage point on this account.[41] When he came to make his own estimates, however, he assumed without comment that the rate of growth from this source was zero.[42]

Crafts also assumed that labour productivity in trade and domestic and personal services did not change between 1801 and 1831. In his early work on the national income estimates for this period, he had shown that the estimate of the rate of economic growth was sensitive to assumptions about productivity in both industry and services.[43] In his later work, Crafts used the growth in employment as a proxy for the growth of output in trade and in domestic and personal services but provided no evidence in support of this procedure. The assumption that trade output grew with employment was defended on the grounds that trade was 'a traditional sector and could be expected to be an area where labour productivity was pretty much constant'. As for domestic and personal services, Crafts said simply that the period 1801 to 1831 was 'short enough . . . for us to believe that productivity in this sector would not be rising'.[44] Deane and Cole's estimates, in contrast, had implied substantial productivity growth in these sectors.

The importance of these assumptions about productivity for Crafts's results can be judged from Table 4.5. Labour productivity is found to have grown much faster in agriculture and in government and the professions than in the rest of the economy. The figure for labour productivity growth in agriculture is the result of subtracting the annual change in the agricultural labour force from Crafts's estimate of the rate of growth of agricultural output.[45] The productivity estimate in agriculture is thus an outcome of the calculations rather than being an ingredient in them. Crafts estimated productivity growth in government and the professions from changes in skilled and unskilled wage rates. Again, an estimate of productivity growth is derived from considering the evidence, though the evidence is indirect.[46] In the remaining sectors distinguished in Table 4.5, the increase in labour productivity is slow and in each of these sectors the estimated rate of productivity growth rests on assumptions which have no evidential basis: the assumption that output per unit of materials input in industry did not change, the assumption that productivity change in transport increased at the same rate as industrial output (including materials) per worker, and the assumption that labour productivity was constant in trade and in domestic and personal services.

Table 4.5 Growth in labour productivity implicit in Crafts's estimates, 1801–31

Sector	% p.a.
Agriculture	0.99
Government and professional	1.37
Industry	0.21
Trade and transport	0.15
Domestic and personal services	0.00

Source: See text

As with the growth estimates for the eighteenth century, the way in which the estimates for the period 1801 to 1831 have been derived limits the uses to which they can be put. Crafts and Harley use the growth estimates to show that both total factor productivity and labour productivity grew more slowly in this period 'than would have been thought with the data used by writers in the 1970s', and they assert that the 'reduced estimates of output growth are the chief reason for this'.[47] The argument of this section would suggest that new data have had little to do with the rise of the revised view. Moreover, the growth accounting exercise which Crafts and Harley pursue involves circular reasoning. It is not surprising that they should find that productivity grew slowly, for the growth estimates to which they appeal effectively assume this to have been so.

CONCLUSION

Deane and Cole were acutely aware that many of their results were 'tentative and questionable' and that they had provided not 'a set of definitive conclusions but a collection of what seemed ... to be consistent (though by no means exhaustive) hypotheses'. Accordingly, they wrote of the 'need for much detailed research at the industrial or regional level before we can confidently describe the quantitative characteristics of British industrialisation'.[48] Much has since been achieved in this direction. The new view of the pace of economic growth during the early phases of industrialization, however, did not emerge from the accumulation of evidence amassed by new research. Rather, the evidence available to Deane and Cole has been looked at in a different way. Crafts's estimates of the rate of growth are the quantitative expression of the new view. In compiling them, he employed both economic theory and ad hoc judgements about what was plausible or probable. The theory and the judgements, however, were based more upon a generalized feeling for what is likely to have been characteristic than upon evidence relating directly to the British economy during the period in question. To this extent, it would appear that Crafts' view of the rate of growth is conditioned by what he expected to see and his growth estimates are not the source of the new view so much as its reflection. As Crafts himself said of the early nineteenth century, our 'estimates of real national output growth . . . are a matter of faith rather than fact'.[49]

5

THE INDUSTRIAL REVOLUTION AND THE GENESIS OF THE MALE BREADWINNER

Stephen Nicholas and Deborah Oxley

INTRODUCTION

Women's status within the family and economy changed with industrialization. Whether the change in status worsened or improved the living standards of women divides historians into optimists and pessimists. For the optimists industrialization enhanced the position and power of women both within the family and the wider socio-economic system by opening up hitherto closed or remote opportunities. Machinery reduced men's strength advantage by minimizing the physical power needed for operation, paid work gave women a choice about remaining unwed, and from the mid-nineteenth century the breadwinning wage freed married women from the burden of earning income while caring for their families. Conversely, the pessimists argued that industrialization replaced a relatively equitable system with one in which women faced fewer employment opportunities than before, received lower wages compared with men, and were increasingly tied by legislation and ideology to gender roles inside and outside the home which impoverished them. Divorced from the labour market advantages held by their brothers and lacking the breadwinning capacities of their husbands, women remained nevertheless responsible for the unpaid and financially unrewarded work of reproduction. Women's status within the family declined.

Neither side in this debate has scored a clear victory, with one recent critic suggesting that resolution is impossible.[1] In this chapter, we offer a resolution of this debate. By suggesting an economic model of how families operate and employing data on the heights of women and men to measure the changing distribution of resources within working-class families, we can judge whether the optimists' or the pessimists' case on the status of women is correct. In Section 2 we trace the debate over the status of women in the family and economy. Section 3 utilizes the recent literature from development economics to derive a model of the economic behaviour of families and shows how heights can be used to measure the well-being of women. The representativeness of our data on heights is discussed in Section 4. In Section 5 data on the heights of 6,296 female convicts are employed to measure women's share of household resources during Britain's Industrial Revolution. A short summary concludes the chapter.

THE DEBATE

Early historical work on industrialization had little to say about women, despite considerable contemporary interest in the topic in the eighteenth and nineteenth centuries.[2] Beyond common stereotypes, women were similarly absent in the writings emanating from the left of the political spectrum up until the 1970s.[3] But while interest was limited, it was not totally absent: two important works came out of the early twentieth century, one by Alice Clark, *Working Life of Women in the Seventeenth Century* (1919) and the other by Ivy Pinchbeck, *Women Workers and the Industrial Revolution* (1930). These two books are classics in the field, for decades remaining the only source on women's work under the influence of capitalism. They also embody the two streams of thought which have come to dominate the debate, with Clark the pessimist and Pinchbeck the optimist.

Clark dated the rise of capitalism, and the demise of women, from the seventeenth century. Prior to capitalism, production in its numerous forms (textile, mining, agriculture) had been based on the employment of families. Employment contracts either explicitly or implicitly entailed that the male worker brought with him his wife and children. Wages reflected this, being payment sufficient to cover the entire family. This interdependence – later labelled 'gynocentric'[4] – conferred some, if not exactly equitable, power on women. By replacing this family unit of production with the nominally 'independent' wage worker, capitalism displaced women from their comparatively powerful position as an integral member of the labour unit. Once trained in their father's or husband's trade, women were excluded from skilled work and increasingly found themselves left out of paid employment more generally. The destruction of the family team left women without paid work and the associated shift from home-based to workshop and factory production for men left women at home with the children. Concomitant with the shift from the family to the individual worker, the wage form was converted from a family payment to one only adequate for the support of an individual. Working-class living standards suffered, but within the working class the onus of the suffering was deeply gendered.

Subsequent historians have challenged Clark's periodization, bringing the date of rapid change into the early-to-mid nineteenth century. Work has progressed from the study of waged employment in industry to include wage-work in agriculture, the changing forms of the family and, increasingly, the continuing economic roles of women in the household or 'non-market' sector. The parts played in the declining status of women by economic necessity, biology, ideology and labour aristocrats have all been considered, with a continuing debate over the relative significance of each. We are now aware that the move into the factory was not a simple and smooth one in which all women were left marooned at home from the start,[5] and we know that there was considerable diversity between single and married women,[6] different occupations,[7] different geographic regions,[8] and, of course, different classes.[9] But while the picture has become far more complicated, Clark's pessimistic line has remained intact, although embellished. That women's position deteriorated has been supported by a wealth of research into census data, parliamentary papers, the evidence of witnesses, detailed studies of household accounts, regional statistics, and newspapers. This new research points to labour market segmentation,[10] disadvantageous wage and training structures,[11] and the loss of common rights closely associated with the work of women and children.[12] These changes held true for women in agriculture, handicraft, and the modern sector. The result was the emergence of the patriarchal family and the appearance of a sustaining ideology. As need became a criterion in determining pay rates, the wage structure based upon the individual earner bifurcated along gender lines. Assumptions regarding masculinity and femininity cemented a male breadwinning wage norm which granted men (irrespective of conjugal status) a superior income to women, based on the assumption that the former and not the latter had dependents to support.[13] When women worked it was assumed to be for pin money.

While Clark's tale was pessimistic, Pinchbeck had a positive story to tell. Pinchbeck focused on the opportunities that industrialization opened up for single urban women. Factories provided jobs with cash payment and a degree of freedom unknown to domestic and farm servants and girls used to working under the close scrutiny of parents. Optimistically, Pinchbeck declared that factories 'meant higher wages, better food and clothing and an improved standard of living. This was especially so in the case of women';[14] and the perils of industry were no more than 'the experience of cottage and workshop industry writ large for all to see'.[15] Married women, too, benefited. Like Clark, Pinchbeck identified the changing wage form as highly significant for women, but her appraisal was favourable. The gradual movement towards a male breadwinning wage meant financial recognition for women's reproductive labours, which freed women from the burden of paid work while acknowledging that 'in the rearing of children and in home-making, the married woman makes an adequate economic contribution'.[16]

Subsequent optimists have advanced a somewhat modified argument. Rather than liberating women from the burden of paid work, the plus of industrialization was to open up the labour market to women. In the pre-industrial past production was heavily dependent upon strength, which disadvantaged women. This, plus domestic responsibilities, fostered a strong division of labour in which women did 'women's work' and men did 'men's work'. Popular culture, religion, and the legal system provided evidence of the low status of women.[17] Industrialization wrought change, to the advantage of women. Machinery reduced the need for physical strength and medical advances reduced the number of pregnancies women needed to bear.[18] Compared with agriculture and domestic service, industry offered women and children more jobs, and they were better paid.[19] The logic of capitalism reduced inequalities. The demand for labour, particularly skilled labour, broke down gender barriers. Facing a more equitable labour market, women increased their bargaining power and status within the family: work and responsibilities were shared more evenly, and the symmetric family triumphed.[20]

Like marriage, was industrialization 'for better or for worse' for women? Where the optimists have found benefits in the transition to capitalism for women, the pessimists have interpreted those same changes as patriarchal and inequitable. For every job that closed down in one area, the optimists pointed to a new job that opened up elsewhere. The debate is fundamentally riddled by two related problems: appropriate data and appropriate indicators. As Thomas notes:

The problem is partly empirical, mainly theoretical. As neither side, the optimists or the pessimists, agree on their criteria for an improvement or deterioration in the position of women, the debate is likely to continue endlessly. Optimists regard the spread of bourgeois freedoms to women, and particularly legislative and political reforms subsequent to industrial capitalism, as sufficient index of their improved status. Pessimists regard these as a mockery in the face of continued discrimination against women in the workplace.[21]

Data are often subjective, and hence subject to dispute over their meaning, or they are quantitative but not directly comparable between pre-industrial and industrial societies. Wages data, the staple source of information on changes in the standard of living, are particularly problematic in the case of women. Wages series for women are not easily found. When wages data can be unearthed they are difficult to compare between regions and over time and are usually limited to women at a specific stage of their life cycle. Furthermore, wages refer only to those women in paid employment and not to females outside the labour market. Finally, wages reveal nothing about how families *allocated* the resources gathered from their members. What is required to resolve this debate over the position of women in the family is information which allows us to *measure* women's share of household resources and their overall well-being relative to men.

Here we propose a way of resolving this persistent debate regarding the changing status of women in the family. We focus on the nature of the transition to capitalism without being committed to a set view of either pre-industrial or industrial society. To test whether the optimists or pessimists are correct, we develop an economic model of how the family works. Specifically, the model specifies that limited resources are allocated according to labour market opportunities and that this allocation reflects status within the family. Secondly, we utilize new data to measure the actual allocation of resources within families during the transitional phase when industrialization was displacing pre-existing socio-economic forms. In addition, we compare what was happening to English women and men during the maelstrom of British industrialization with their contemporaries in Ireland, a country *not* undergoing such changes, where pre- and proto-industrial family relations remained intact.

THE MODEL AND METHOD

Economic models of the family, and their quantitative verification, offer one way to answer questions about the changing status and role of women in the workforce and family during industrialization. Economic theory depicts the family as an economic and social unit where controlling family members determine the allocation of household resources vital to their children's future standard of living.[22] Food, essential for strength needed to perform labour-intensive work, and schooling are fundamental for the physical and 'human capital' development of children. The concept of human capital was first developed by Adam Smith in the *Wealth of Nations* when he compared an educated person to an expensive machine. Like a machine, an educated person who has invested in schooling or training receives a higher wage over their lifetime than a person without schooling. Similarly, well fed men and women earn higher incomes than poorly fed workers since they can work longer hours at harder tasks and can better resist diseases which reduce work capacity. Our model of the family posits that parents allocate scarce nutrients and education between competing family members in order to maximize total household economic returns in the long run. For these families, the allocation of intrahousehold resources between children will depend on gender differences in expected labour market outcomes.

There exists substantial empirical evidence from today's developing countries to support this model of intrahousehold resource allocation. We know that labour market returns to men and women diverge as developing economies shift from subsistence to market-based production. The higher economic value families place on males *vis-à-vis* females is related to the greater ability of men to support parents in their old age, the higher labour force participation of boys and men, and the greater earning power of men.[23] This gender-based differential in expected labour market returns has led to a pro-male distribution of nutrients and education within the family in many developing countries.[24]

The pro-male bias has been revealed in weight-by-age and height-by-age data which show a systematic sex bias in malnutrition, with a higher nutrient deprivation for girls than boys.[25] Survey and econometric estimation found that household members claimed extra food when their occupations required high levels of calories and paid work took place outside the home. During industrialization, it was the males who increasingly found outside work and males who were hired for labour-intensive tasks.[26] This pro-male labour market advantage was reflected in the much sharper gender discrimination in the allocation of food in a sample of Indian and Pakistani villages with the best over-all nutritional record. It was in these better-fed villages where market forces and land reform had proceeded furthest and where employment opportunities for women had declined most.[27]

This contemporary evidence confirms that height, weight, and food intake are reliable measures of the changing status of women during the transition from subsistence agricultural to market-based production. Until now historical data on women's nutrition precluded strong claims about the changing home and work experience of English women during the early years of the British Industrial Revolution. Auxology, the study of human growth, and new data on the heights of 6,296 convict women transported before 1840, provide a new way for analysing the changing position of women in the labour force and family during industrialization.

Human biologists, anthropologists, and nutritionalists have found that measures of stature are a sensitive indicator of a population's changing average nutritional status and living standards.[28] In a sample of developed and underdeveloped countries, average height was found to be highly correlated with per capita incomes, which suggests that factors correlated with poverty, such as poor diet, hard work, and poor medical care, were major sources of nutritional deprivation and slow human growth.[29] There is good evidence that war-time shortages of food can slow growth and disease may also retard growth by impeding the absorption of nutrients and diverting nutrition to combat infection. Malnutrition and illness may interact to produce an effect larger than the separate effects of each in isolation.[30] Food intake and the disease environment impact on the change in height between successive ages (velocity or growth spurt), the age at which final height is reached and final adult height, which mean that height provides a reliable index of women's changing well-being. Among historians it is now widely accepted that height data offer a reliable measure of living standards, superior to wages data which measure one source of income and reveal nothing about expenditure.[31]

As a measure of living standards, all these height indexes are net rather than gross measures of nutrition. Height depends not only on the nutrition available for human growth but also on the claims made on nutrients for body maintenance given work intensity, the disease environment, and the state of public health. The heights of convict women were the outcome both of their share of the food available in the household and their exposure to the external work and living environment during their growing years. For convicts, the growing years lasted until age 21 for females and age 23 for males. Cohort data on height are presented by year of birth, since it is not possible to determine during what periods in the convict's growing years environmental insults or 'good times' occurred, or when work demands and the allotment of food had their greatest effect on stature.

Our data on heights include observations on both English-born and Irish-born women. Ireland acts as a control economy. Of course Ireland was not simply England without an industrial revolution, but contemporary observers and historians have often looked to Ireland to see what would have happened to the English economy without an industrial revolution. Backward and agrarian, Ireland remained firmly set in the pattern of a pre-industrial subsistence economy little touched by the dramatic changes transforming England into a market-based capitalist economy. Comparing the trends in heights of women in England and Ireland provides one measure of the impact of industrialization on the living standards of English women.

THE DATA

Our information on the heights of women growing up during British industrialization is unique. Historians using height data to discuss male living standards have exploited army recruitment records, but no comparable register existed for women. However, when women broke the criminal code, they entered into a legal bureaucracy which documented them in considerable detail. Data on 2,926 English-born and 3,370 Irish-born women were taken from the lists or Indents which accompanied all female convicts transported to New South Wales between 1826 and 1840. Convict Indents enumerated each convict's height, age, occupations, county of birth (including rural or urban location), county of trial, crime, sentence, and previous convictions. Comparative data on 12,528 English and 7,358 Irish males transported between 1817 and 1840 were also analysed.

Our first concern was whether the data on heights displayed any truncation problems related to only tall or short women and men being selected for transportation. Inspections of the height distributions revealed no shortfalls or overloading of the tails of the distributions which would indicate selection bias on the basis of height. The male and female height data were all normally distributed, but the rural Irish and English female height distributions displayed heaping at the full and half inch.[32] While not a desirable quality, heaping affects many studies of height, including modern ones, and simulations show that heaping on the full and half-inch is a relatively minor adverse effect in the estimation of mean heights because their effects are largely self-cancelling.[33]

To establish the representativeness of our data, information on over 160 different female occupations in the Indents was used to assess from what part of the population our female transportees were selected.[34] Female employment fell mainly into a dozen categories,[35] with 65 per cent of the women employed as housemaids, all workers, or kitchenhands at some point prior to their transportation. Occupations were coded into 5 categories using Armstrong's social class/skill scheme: 1 – professional; 2 – middling; 3 – skilled; 4 – semiskilled; and 5 – unskilled.[36] Half the convict women were skilled workers, with the remaining women roughly split between semiskilled and unskilled work.

Unfortunately, the skill composition of working women in the 1841 English census could not be easily compared with that of our sample of female convicts because half of all working women in the census were lumped into one amorphous 'domestic servant' category. Domestic service occupations included both skilled and semiskilled jobs, forcing us to aggregate Armstrong's skilled and semiskilled categories into one general skill category. This aggregate category included 78 per cent of the convict and 83 per cent of the English census females. By this test, the female convicts were as skilled as the working women left at home.

From the detailed information on occupations available in the Indents (but not in the 1841 English census), our sample probably somewhat over-represented the number of domestic servants and agricultural workers and under-represented the proportion of textile workers. This arose, in part, from the age distribution of convict women, who were disproportionately young (with 75 per cent of the English and 79 per cent of the Irish below the age of 31). Our data show that with increasing age the number of women employed in domestic service fell from 82.4 per cent for young English convict women (that is, under 20 years of age) to 68 per cent of women over the age of 20. Employment in domestic service required women to be single and the high percentage of unmarried women among the transportees (59 per cent of the English and 65 per cent of the Irish convict women were single) also explains the high percentage of domestic servants in our sample.

To test for selection biases in the Irish data, female convict occupations and occupations in the 1841 Irish census were both coded using six broad occupational categories devised by Mokyr and O'Grada in their study of Irish emigrants to Boston using shipping lists.[37] The 1841 Irish census grouped women into two major job categories, labourers (34 per cent) and textile workers (60 per cent), while the female convicts were classified in the Indents as labourers (92 per cent). The same tendency to group female occupations into the labourer–servant category (79 per cent) also affected the Boston emigrant data. These apparent differences disappear once it is remembered that female textile workers in the census were listed as farm servants (or labourers) in the Indents and shipping lists because they worked at home as domestic workers. On the basis of their occupational skills, it appears that the women transported from Ireland were broadly coincident with the working-class population at home.

Information on literacy was also used to assess the representativeness of our female convict data. The female convicts and the population at home had similar levels of literacy. Less than half of the English women marrying between 1825 and 1840 signed the marriage register; 45 per cent of the convict women tried in England could read and a further 35 per cent could write also. In terms of literacy skills, the female convicts (80 per cent could read and/or write) were more like free English women migrants to Australia (79 per cent could read and/or write) than English paupers (only 33 per cent could read and/or write). From the 1841 Irish census, 45 per cent of the Irish women and 48 per cent of the convict women could read and/or write, suggesting that the transported Irish women and the female population left in Ireland were basically similar on educational grounds.

Our claim that the transported women were broadly representative of the English and Irish working class gains additional support from recent historical work on crime and criminals. While not 'honest men and women', this work concluded that the convicts were usually people in employment, who supplemented their incomes by theft during times of distress.[38] The criminals transported to Australia were not a class apart from ordinary working-class men and women. A majority of the female transportees had no prior convictions. Most crimes involved the theft of small or inexpensive articles, predominantly at the expense of employers and masters.[39] On the basis of all these tests, it seems fair to conclude that the women convicts in our sample were broadly representative of working-class women in Britain and Ireland.

FEMALE AND MALE HEIGHTS

The timing and amplitude of the adolescent growth spurt are sensitive both to nutritional factors and the external environment, providing one measure of female living standards during the early Industrial Revolution. As can be seen in Figure 5.1, English women experienced their growth spurt from about age 14 until age 16.5 or 17.5. It began later and lasted about four years longer than that of well-nourished girls today, whose spurt begins at age 10.5 and continues until age 13.[40] The later spurt for convict girls meant that terminal height for English women was attained at age 21, well beyond the modern average of about age 17. The delayed and much longer growth spurt of English women was also typical of the growth pattern of English males, who spurted between the ages of 14 and 15 (one year later than for well-nourished boys today) and continued to grow until age 23 (three years beyond the modern standard of age 19). The delayed and dampened spurt, which was also experienced by Irish-born girls, meant that women and men both suffered from some combination of poor food allotments, environmental insults, and adverse work demands during their growing years.

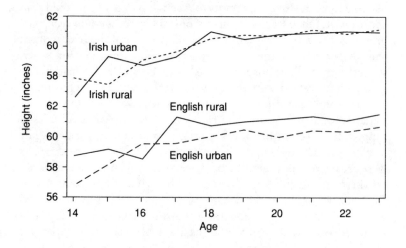

Figure 5.1 Height by age of English and Irish females

Table 5.1 Terminal height and T-test for differences in terminal heights

	English rural	English urban	Irish rural	Irish urban
		Females		
Height (inches)	61.65	60.75	61.29	61.14
English rural		10.71*	5.71*	4.18*
English urban			8.44*	3.68*
Irish rural				0.73
		Males		
Height (inches)	65.96	65.44	66.10	65.82
English rural		7.12*	1.94	1.39
English urban			8.16*	3.57*
Irish rural				1.09

Note: * Significant at 0.05
Source: Author's work on data extracted from Convict Indents

But English women and men did not suffer equally. Calculating terminal heights in Table 5.1, urban-born women were nearly one inch shorter than their rural sisters, while urban-born men were only half an inch shorter than their rural brothers. But the urban-born experienced the same urban disamenities, irrespective of their gender. This suggests that nutritional factors, not environmental ones, explain the much poorer growth performance of women compared with men during England's Industrial Revolution.

The poor growth performance of English women is highlighted in the 5-year moving averages of female terminal height in Figure 5.2. While Figure 5.2 confirms the persistent and significant difference in the height of urban and rural English women, this differential is of less significance than the downward trend in female heights. From a peak of 61.75 inches in the late 1790s, the height of female birth cohorts born in rural England fell continuously to just under 61 inches by the end of the Napoleonic wars. The heights of urban-born women fell slightly, ending the period about a quarter of an inch below their pre-1800 level.

Male heights also fell after 1795. But the heights of rural women fell significantly faster than those of rural men. Beginning the century at 61.75 inches, rural women's heights fell to under 61 inches for cohorts born in 1815; in contrast, rural male cohorts were only one quarter of an inch shorter in 1815 (65.75 inches) than in 1800 (66 inches). The heights of urban women fell about the same as those for urban males.

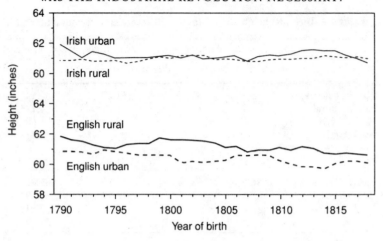

Figure 5.2 Height profiles, English and Irish females (5-year moving average for ages 21–49 years)

The similar trends in the heights of urban women and men is what might be expected when both sexes were subject to the same environmental impacts and had equivalent access to nutrients. Since rural women were subject to the same environmental forces as rural men, the gender differences in the trend of rural female and male heights must be due to differences in the quality of the diet and/or the allocation of food within the family household.

The more rapid fall in rural-born women's heights compared with the urban-born eliminates the *quality* of the diet as the cause of the widening differential between the heights of rural English men and women. War, blockade, and harvest failure meant deficient food inputs for both men and women, reflected in the similar fluctuations in the downward movement in the moving averages of terminal height for both sexes after the mid-1790s. Further, rural women had *better* access to food supplies during blockade and harvest short-fall than those living in towns, and the quality of the urban diet – store-bought and frequently adulterated – was inferior to the rural diet.[41] For these reasons alone urban heights should have fallen relative to rural heights. The fall after 1795 in rural women's heights relative to urban women and rural men must have been due to a shrinking share of the family's scarce food supplies allotted to women living in the countryside.

Height data indicates that women's claim on household resources was declining and this is confirmed by our evidence on literacy. Education is an investment in human capital budgeted by households between family members and relative to other inputs such as food, clothing, and medical services. According to Burnett, what the English labouring family spent on bacon, beer, and white bread was spent by the Scottish family on the education of their children.[42] Women had poorer access to schooling. Signature tests in the marriage register show that women had lower levels of literacy than men and, from a list of the inhabitants of Cardington in 1792, Schofield found that boys typically attended school until age 11 while girls had only a 1:3 chance of schooling.[43] Figure 5.3 presents five-year moving averages of literacy for our females which throws new light on the trend in female literacy during industrialization. Both rural and urban English females experienced decreasing literacy from 1795. The tendency for heights and literacy to move together suggests that when households reduced their expenditure on food intake they also invested less in expensive schooling.

All this information indicates that English women, particularly those born in rural locations, suffered a decline in their share of household resources during industrialization. In particular, there are two notable features in the height profiles of the English. Firstly, the poor growth experience of industrial revolution women depended, in part, on birthplace. At maturity, urban-born women were significantly shorter than the rural-born; the same held true for men,

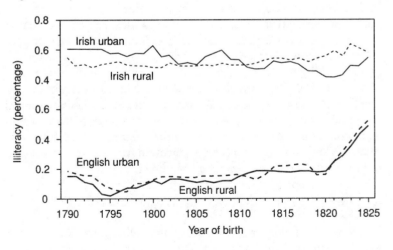

Figure 5.3 Illiteracy of English and Irish females (5-year moving average)

although there the extent of the difference was not as great (see Table 5.1). Secondly, and more significantly, during industrialization rural women lost their height advantage: not because urban women grew in stature, but because the heights of rural women fell dramatically. Women's heights fell because the share of household nutrients allocated to girls declined. We argue that women claimed a declining share of household resources because industrialization curtailed women's employment opportunities in the paid labour market. As it was country women who faced the most disadvantageous labour market,[44] it was English country women who suffered the greatest deprivation – a finding supported by recent work into female differential mortality. The countryside was hostile to female life chances, 'not because it traditionally afforded few productive opportunities for women, but because it had been transformed and, in the process, female employment and self employment almost eliminated'.[45]

This poor nutritional experience of English women and the divergence between urban and rural experiences (reflected in the terminal heights in Table 5.1 and also evident in Figure 5.1) contrasts sharply with what was happening to women in the traditional economy of Ireland. While English women's stature fell, Figure 5.2 shows that the height of Irish women improved, rising about 0.5 inches for Irish urban women and about 0.25 inches for the rural-born. Rural Irish women began the period shorter than the rural English, but had gained a significant height advantage over the English by 1812. Urban Irish women increased their height advantage over the English. Backward agricultural Ireland maintained a higher nutritional level for its urban women than wealthier England. In terms of literacy, Figure 5.3 shows that urban Irish women improved their level of literacy, while Ireland's rural women's literacy was much the same in 1820 as in 1800. Untouched by the industrialization process transforming England, the traditional Irish peasant family allocated intrahousehold resources roughly equally. Women were partners with men, both at home as managers of children and household financial resources and at work in paid employment. In Ireland, women's share of intrahousehold resources did not decline.

CONCLUSIONS

What does all this information on resource allocation mean for the genesis of the male breadwinner? The male breadwinning wage was conceived as a payment sufficient for a man to support his dependent wife and children. Conversely, as dependents, women and children required lower wages. The emergence of this ideology and associated wage norm are dated from the middle of the nineteenth century – the only point on which the optimists and the pessimists agree.[46] Optimists hailed the development of the male breadwinner as recognition of women's unpaid labours. Pessimists perceived the opposite dynamic, with the male breadwinning wage norm cementing men and women into gender roles unknown in pre-industrial times, instituting female dependence on men. Our data support the pessimist case, but place the emergence of the male breadwinner half a century earlier.

Hilary Land tells us that the individual male wage-worker benefitted from the new wage norm:

> As breadwinner he was able to claim a larger share of the food. Adopting the ideal of the family wage earned by the strength and efforts of the male breadwinner ensured that the long-standing custom of giving priority to the nutritional needs of the male adults in the household was not challenged in the social and economic upheavals of the nineteenth century.[47]

We found a pro-male bias in the allocation of household resources by the late eighteenth century that not only failed to be challenged as time progressed, but which intensified. It intensified because industrialization opened up different labour market opportunities for men than for women. We argue that industrialization broke the existing nexus between work, power, status, and access to resources. Once marginalized within the paid labour market women's power, status, and access to resources within the family were promptly reduced. The dramatic fall in women's height after 1800 stands as testimony to the speed and magnitude of the fall in women's status with industrialization. While the male breadwinning wage norm might not have been clearly articulated until later in the century, household economies were already functioning on this basis half a century earlier. Industrialization ushered in new and gendered economic roles and their impact upon family relationships was felt immediately.

6

THE INDUSTRIAL REVOLUTION REVISITED

Stanley L. Engerman

The chapters in this volume deal with rather diverse themes, but all are concerned with some aspect of Britain in the period of the Industrial Revolution. It will, therefore, be useful to discuss each chapter separately, before adding some general reflections on where these revisits have left the study of the topic. The discussion will seem, at times, rather diverse since these chapters represent only a small part of extended research projects of the authors. Nevertheless, each chapter, on its own, makes a substantial contribution to the economic and social history of the period.

I

E. A. Wrigley's chapter can be divided into two parts. One is related to his ongoing work dealing with the role and nature of energy in the Industrial Revolution. The other part deals with the perceptions of leading contemporaries of the Industrial Revolution, the classical economists, and their discussions of the causes and consequences of all of those happenings. It will be easiest for me to regard this as two interrelated papers.

The need, or at least use, of coal as a source of energy to provide for sustained, rapid economic growth, in England and elsewhere in Europe, has long been noted. Perhaps coal was less essential in the early stages of growth in England's former colony in North America, the United States, where water and wood were prime energy sources in the years before the Civil War, but some debate remains as to how long this pattern could have been sustained without the expanded use of coal. Wrigley's argument as to the central importance of coal to most developed nations is clearly reasonable, particularly given doubts as to the possible pace of technological change using the other then available sources of energy and the probable delays, at any set of relative prices, in the discovery and use of those new sources that would ultimately drive out coal. Neither of these possibilities for effective substitutes for coal seems historically relevant, even within rather imaginative counterfactual worlds.

The one question remaining is why, given the earlier knowledge of the existence of coal, it took so long before it was so heavily utilized. Was it due to a change in the knowledge about the use of coal, or was it due to a change in tastes regarding economic improvement which led to the greater use of coal? The British did use coal earlier than elsewhere on the continent and began its extended use at a time when their energy needs seemed less than they would ultimately become. Thus coal may not just explain the British Industrial Revolution, but also an early British jump on the rest of the continent in the period preceding the onset of industrialization. In any event, this focus on the key importance of coal does return us to earlier contentions of British advantage, linking its natural resource base with its economic development and attributing the slower movements in follower nations to their resource limitations.

Wrigley's discussion of the classical economists makes two important related points. First, they did clearly note some of the key changes made at the time. Second, they did, however, expect and predict the re-emergence of stagnation and the stationary state. On this latter point it would be interesting to learn more about how long they perceived the time to re-achieve stagnation (whether in total or per capita income) would be. Was it rather imminent, say, within their lifetimes, or off sometime in a distant future? Gibbon had described the Byzantine part of the Roman Empire as having a 1300 years steady decline before its final collapse. Did the classical economists' logic relate to a shorter, but still considerable, time in the future?

This last question arises because several nineteenth-century economists did concern themselves with the possible disappearance of Britain's cheap coal. Charles Babbage, in 1832, believed that coal might run out, but that it would be replaced by alternative sources of energy. William Stanley Jevons, writing in 1865, made economic forecasts for Britain based on expectations as to what would happen to the available stock of coal, predicting a British decline in economic power to occur in about one century. This forecast was updated by his son fifty years later, but the period over which the coal problem would be manifested was now seen as two centuries. Even with a knowledge of coal as the key source of power, the Jevonses – father and son –

could still argue for a return to no-growth and a loss of British power. This was obviously on the basis of more information and statistics than were used by Smith, Malthus, or Ricardo. Thus the Jevonses may have had a better perception of their present world, but it remains uncertain that, in these matters regarding the future, they had a better knowledge of the causes and consequences of economic change.

II

Graeme Snooks, in Chapter 3, is concerned with the measure of very long-term economic growth, based upon his earlier work on Domesday Book, using the estimated patterns of growth to draw implications for the nature of economic society prior to the Industrial Revolution. These, in turn, serve to provide some understanding of what, if any, were the basic changes that occurred in the period of what many still call the Industrial Revolution. His basic argument is that growth has long existed in England, at least, since less is directly said about changes elsewhere. And, since many scholars have not often fully accepted this argument about long-term economic change, its causes have not really been examined in appropriate detail.

The key measures underlying Snooks's findings are those for national income in 1086 derived, in part, from Domesday Book (adjusted to allow for the subsistence income of about two-thirds of the population, utilizing indirect measures) and that of Gregory King for 1688, accepted with the allowances made by Lindert and Williamson for earlier criticisms raised concerning King's procedures and conclusions. For the post-1688 period, use is made of the various national income estimates familiar to all economic historians. For years between 1086 and 1688, Snooks uses simulations based on several economic and demographic variables to provide estimates for various sub-periods. Little direct is said about the precise simulation procedures here, so more attention at present will be given to the implications of these estimates than to their accuracy. It should be noted that little is said about possible economic growth before 1086 and the possible achievement of above-subsistence levels of income for workers by that year.

There are some familiar and some unexpected patterns seen in Snooks's simulations. There is a sharp decline in per capita income with the Black Death, but, even with a period of slow and limited recovery, the per capita income of 1492 still remained below the mid-twelfth-century level. Indeed, given the contention of long-term growth, it should be noted that it is the post-1492 expansion (an expansion that did not surprise Adam Smith) that accounts for most of the growth between 1086 and 1688, although, it might be noted, the growth rate between 1086 and 1170 was high by any pre-1800 standard. The 'great waves' idea, as applied to this period, sees one long cycle, with a sharp expansion and decline, and then dramatic change after the start of the sixteenth century. And, with all this early change, it remains that about 90 per cent of the increase in per capita income between 1086 and 1987 occurred in the last two centuries, after 1800.

The simulation of per capita income appears to track, positively, population growth. Growth was also generally higher in periods called inflationary (actually of high absolute wheat prices), another old historiographic theme, but there is no monetary argument presented. The positive relation of population and per capita income growth is similar to that in most cases of modern economic growth (except Ireland). Thus its occurrence may not be particularly surprising, given the recent frequency, but it remains that the key argument is whether such a prolonged positive relation was possible only after the eighteenth century. In any event, Snooks has launched an attack on those claiming a Malthusian-like inverse relation of population and per capita income over long periods of time as the historical standard. While the Malthusian argument, based on limited resources and diminishing returns, has long been a favourite of medieval economic historians (and actually does reasonably well in Snooks's estimation for short periods after 1300 and, again, after 1650), a positive relation between population and economic growth has at least two different sets of possible causal connections. To the economic historian of the longrun arguments derived from Adam Smith and from Allyn Young point to the impact of increased population size in permitting economies of scale from the division of labour. Less useful for any longrun analysis, but still sometimes discussed, is a Keynesian-like impact upon aggregate demand and resource utilization. A counter to these arguments is one posed by Habakkuk, who sees low population and labour scarcity generating pressure to seek breakthroughs in new technologies or new resource discoveries, thus having a smaller population led to more rapid growth. Thus the relations of population and economic activity are seldom simple, and, as part of the sketch of development over time, it would be interesting to disentangle the various explanatory factors.

I do think, however, that Snooks has understated the historiographic importance of the Malthusian argument used by earlier scholars to describe the presumed path of economic change in England. The impact of the argument seems considerably more important in explaining what historians believed than were the quantitative calculations of Phelps Brown and Hopkins. It is more probable that people found their estimates believable because they get the Malthusian predictions, not vice versa. Most of the arguments criticized by Snooks are premised on the law of diminishing returns in a predominantly agricultural economy, with presumably limited possible change in technology and in land and labour productivity.

Yet that argument, the core of the postulated inverse relation of population change and economic change, even if correct for some hypothetical longrun, may be of some limited use for the historical periods discussed. Sometimes the presentation of the argument attacked by Snooks contains a confusion between the existence of a new equilibrium and the length of time and nature of the output path to get there. Thus, for example, discussions of the period of frontier expansion in the centuries prior to the economic decline of the Black Death often seem to focus on the move from one equilibrium to another, putting aside the changes in the long period which passed before the Malthusian problems reasserted themselves. Looked at this way, discussions of earlier periods of rapid growth were not absent from the literature, but they did get lost in the collapsing of centuries to focus on the population-created economic dilemmas.

Most observers would, however, agree with much of Snooks's analysis. Clearly, by 1700, England had a relatively high level of per capita income and wealth and was in an excellent position to seek the next stage of economic growth. Suggestions on this point have been derived from trade statistics, town developments, and industrial development, as well as from discussions of investment magnitudes by Postan and others pointing to the magnitude of cathedral construction. What is at issue in these debates is the pre-1700 pattern, which poses certain sets of problems no matter what is said about earlier levels of income and pre-1700 rates of economic growth. In this sense the broad outlines presented by Snooks do seem more plausible, for if one maintains scepticism about the earlier rates of growth, then high levels of income for England at any earlier stage must be accepted. It seems more probable, therefore, that pre-1700 growth must have occurred and, even if there were great waves, on net the long-term movement was upward. But if the issue is when did modern, prolonged, continuous, and rapid growth begin, the familiar answer would seem to be that something at the start of the nineteenth century led to a dramatic and prolonged shift upward in growth rates, although the preceding centuries did have some relatively lengthy periods of high growth. The nature of economic growth seemed to differ before and after the watershed of the Napoleonic wars. The subsequent almost two centuries of growth at relatively high rates represent a new stage in the historical record, although one that may, perhaps, become damped in future years, giving Snooks another 'great wave' movement.

Snooks's contributions to a second debate are also certain to provide some extensive historical discussions. Arguing from the existence of high rates of economic growth, Snooks claims that this was no accident and that there was an economic man (person?) who was rational before modern times. The general point seems, again, quite plausible, since people no doubt did seek economic betterment, if only for their long-period survival, but it is not clear that we can regard the growth that occurred as maximal or optimal, characteristics which some might think implicit in the description of economic man. Thus some questions remain. What was he (or she) out to maximize in their behaviour: income; a mix of income and leisure; power and control over labour; military power; a mix of income with relaxation, light labour intensity, and few hours worked? The nature of the utility-giving variables that go into the maximization might have been rather large and their achievement may not always go to maximize measured individual or national income. Further, given these individual attempts at maximizing something, we must also consider what 'society' permitted. Did social laws and institutions and/or elite control operate to offset or limit the impact of potential impediments to growth, and how were institutions constructed to minimize conflicts among individuals and groups? Could it have been too costly to society's resources to end conflict and limit impediments to growth, thus permitting some growth but not the full amount that might have seemed possible? Thus the world of political man might not have been one that produced the best outcome for economic man.

III

Robert Jackson presents another aspect of his ongoing work evaluating the construction and the implications of measures of eighteenth- and nineteenth-century United Kingdom conventionally measured market-type output, as well as the various interpretations of the growth experience that they generate. His chapter in this volume is primarily concerned with the estimation of overall output levels in the period including the Industrial Revolution. The principal issue is the frequent need to utilize proxies for various components of output, since we lack the type of direct data we would get from census returns and tax records. Jackson's central concern is the precise use of proxies and the way in which determining their contribution to output depends upon a specific set of assumptions, even when these assumptions are based upon some available information relating to the structure of the economy, either for the period estimated or for some other period. As Jackson shows, the outcome of the use of these proxies can be rather complex and any evaluation of biases uncertain, since often the nature of allocations for different sectors are inter-related and not all the biases obviously go in the same direction (assuming that we can even figure out the direction of bias for any one component). Proxies used in estimating sectoral output levels and trends have been numerous and diverse, including use of estimated relative levels of productivity change in different sectors, a simple link to the expansion of population, or (as done by Deane and Cole in an important estimate) using the change in foreign trade to set the growth pattern for various industries.

While Jackson points to the problems arising owing to the need to use indirect measures to estimate output, many of the problems he points to are general to estimates of national income even when there are more direct measures of outputs and inputs. There is always an index number problem in preparing estimates of output in constant prices or in assigning weights for the estimation of aggregate outputs from sub-sector measures, where the measures of aggregate rate of change will vary with the specific year chosen to provide the price or the quantity weights. There is, unfortunately, no one correct answer to this problem, since, as Kuznets pointed out, the choice of any one year for measurement means the implicit selection of a particular year's estimator to evaluate the magnitude of economic change over time. Similarly, some basic problems of measuring national income persist even with full production and input data and when the basic rules for conventionally measuring national income are agreed to. As the recent literature on the computer and other producer and consumer durables has indicated, the definition of a commodity is not always simple to accomplish. There are issues in allocations of the service and the government sectors when the industrial structure changes and when outputs and inputs shift between market and non-market activity. Multiple occupations for labour have long existed, and the precise allocation of labour and its output to sectors when measuring aggregate output has elements of uncertainty. In general, conventional measures of national income have difficulties in defining the magnitude of non-market activities and in handling such externalities as environmental change and neighbourhood effects.

Thus, all growth of national income estimates, and not just those forced to rely on proxies, are based upon conventions more or less generally agreed upon. Are the need for and variety of different assumptions used in the reworking of old and indirect evidence really that different from those based directly on new and more direct evidence? In most cases the basic test for any measure is the consistency of the calculation with other available evidence and the plausibility of those specific assumptions which are always needed. And this is not just for the preparation of economic time series, being a problem of any historical study, quantitative or non-quantitative, and, indeed, of any type of study attempting to draw conclusions from the vast reality. In the studies analysed by Jackson, estimation was based upon a number of perceived assumptions applied to specific sectors, and the overall estimates are the outcome of many, frequently unrelated, sets of assumptions which, if they cannot provide a precise, agreed-upon estimate, may at least be used to set plausibility bounds for the estimates made.

Jackson's revisions do change some of the patterns seen in the presently widely accepted estimates, but some basic patterns of change central to debates on the Industrial Revolution remain. Under most of the alternatives Jackson presents, relative growth rates in the different sub-periods are still generally ranked the same, as are the relative growth rates for the different sectors. By most of the reasonable measures he presents, there is still some acceleration in the British growth rate of per capita income in the period from the late eighteenth to the early nineteenth century. Yet there is some smoothing away of any overly dramatic late-eighteenth-century acceleration, and acceleration remains less sharp than in the earliest Deane and Cole estimates. It might be noted that this shifting to a slightly later dating of growth acceleration does accord better with what we now know about the pattern of demographic change. While this takes away some of the drama of an eighteenth-century acceleration considered as the Industrial Revolution, maybe it is a useful reminder that, as often argued, structural change and modernization might first emerge in a small segment of the economy and at not quite so rapid rates at the start as those that will emerge later. Nevertheless, while the impact on aggregate measured growth may at first be slow, such changes are necessary for what will come later and in other sectors.

IV

The chapter by Stephen Nicholas and Deborah Oxley concerns certain aspects of the ongoing debate about changes in the standard of living during the period of the Industrial Revolution, here dealing primarily with its effects upon women. It represents a continuation of some of their ongoing research, some published jointly, some separately, using data on height and literacy obtained from the records of convicts sent from England and Ireland to Australia in the nineteenth century. These data are used to examine the changing welfare of women in the years of industrialization. The convict data are particularly useful for such purposes, since they are one of the few sources which provide information on heights for a large number of females.

The analysis presented by Nicholas and Oxley is a quite interesting one – a big issue, the changing role of women, is to be examined with the use of a rather nice, narrow data source. In some ways, however, the use of the data without many other relevant sources may lead to a rather inappropriately sharply defined answer to a broader question. It might lead one to believe that the answer to the question, 'did the position of women improve during the Industrial Revolution?', can be given as simply yes or no, rather than there being a mixed answer depending upon the dimensions asked about, whether we are asking about a specific short-term period or allowing for a full set of longrun responses, and, in general, how we interpret the mixed-set of influences leading to any pattern of behaviour. There are also issues of how changes in any time period can be interpreted, since the changes over time may not be simply linear and the trend not easily extrapolated backward or forward. Changing economic and social structures may lead to different effects over time, and to fully understand the British case it would be useful to have a better grasp of what is happening elsewhere at the same time. Given the large size of the population discussed, and given the not very dramatic magnitudes of relative changes in heights and literacy rates which are the base of the argument, is there any way to translate percentage changes into measures of changes in overall status, and how do we make meaningful comparisons over time?

As the authors point out, heights can provide a measure of net nutrition. The definition of net nutrition is often important, since it means allowances must be made for changing work effort and for the impact of the disease environment, health care, and related factors that influence the relation between gross nutritional input and achieved height. Thus it may be that more nutrition and harder work will leave the same outcome as less nutrition and less intense work, and that some exogenous changes in the disease environment (at whatever ages they may be argued to influence achieved height) might lead to declines in height for some periods, even with increased gross nutrition and unchanged labour effort. Work here might mean either in market activities or within the household, or both, but within the present debate these might be interpreted differently for other reasons.

In extrapolating from the sample of convict women to the broader population of British women, it is useful to note that most studied were of ages which meant they were not married or at many types of industrial, market work. Thus it is not clear how representative these unmarried, non-industrial labouring women are in regard to those members of society for whom the big questions are asked, however appropriate a sample they might represent for other questions. Longer periods of study may be useful to compare patterns of fertility change, family size, and survival rates (absolute as well as relative). There is also a question to ask on whether the argued-for gender effects were deliberately desired by the mass of male society (or perhaps imposed by the male elite), or the unexpected side-effect of some set of policies undertaken for other purposes. If the former, one is curious as to the absence of any real suggestion of a Chinese solution – female infanticide – to more clearly achieve this goal.

The specifics of what height can be safely assumed to measure, and what relatively small differences over time might indicate, remain puzzling, particularly as more information on the historical record has been generated. What effect, for example, is due to exogenous disease shocks to which the body responds, a point that might be critical in a period that includes the Napoleonic wars and the turmoil in their aftermath. Nutrition is a measure of food input, not of total income or consumption, so that change in tastes and relative prices may influence the food input from any level of income. People do not behave, usually, to maximize their height and nutritional input, as suggested by changing heights in rural areas when opened to trade and as seen in urban–rural comparisons at that time, as well as in the

English–Irish comparisons. When people can sell newly expensive food and shift their consumption patterns, their food consumption and their overall consumption may move in different directions. And how are we to evaluate the implied Irish trade-off, of greater gender equality for the dramatic impact of the Famine within a few years, as a long-term solution, whatever other sources may lead us to believe about other aspects of gender relations within Ireland? There is also a sense in which, disappointingly, the analysis of heights presents a problem similar to that which has long influenced studies of wage patterns. The sensitivity to the choice of starting and ending years can often have a dramatic effect on the outcome and, within the discussion of the standard of living in the Industrial Revolution debate, the inclusion or exclusion of the Napoleonic war years may leave an impact. As Nicholas and Oxley show elsewhere, a small extension of the period covered can influence the interpretation, suggesting that the results here may not be as robust as we would like. It is, of course, possible that any of these various types of exogenous shocks mentioned would affect males and females equally, but this could still leave some measures unclear and raise issues of the timing of changes for both sexes.

The issue of household power is seen in the discussion of the concept of the family wage, a debate quite similar to that which emerged in the United States at a later time. The family wage idea was not to claim that women deserved little in the economy, but more to argue that the male should be able to earn enough to provide for his family and thus to permit (what was considered a good thing at that time) women to reduce their market labour. It was claimed that single females still in their original households would need less income, the family wage issue being used to justify low wages for them, particularly if it was expected to be only a temporary period in the market labour force. Nevertheless, nothing about the family wage says anything directly about the specific allocation of consumption within the household to its various members. If women in previous periods had the receipt of market wages, these may have gone into the family pot and been divided in a manner similar to that when males were the sole providers to the household. Immigrant children in the US who, by culture, contributed to their parents' household, did not necessarily, because of labour, draw more from the household coffers than did the non-workers. Intra-family redistributions have always been a tricky matter, and it is obvious that all housework and childcare of females has been financially rewarded for a rather long time even if not directly within what might be regarded as the market sphere. To examine this issue fully it remains necessary to study the actual intra-family allocations, since the family wage itself could permit any split of consumption goods within the household, and the allocation of consumption (of food or also of other goods) need not follow the same breakdown as that of earnings – indeed it seldom does within any family or other social unit.

V

These revisits to the Industrial Revolution are based, as are all such revisits, on some combination of newly available data, new analysis of previously available data, new interpretations of old data, and new insights based upon observations relating not only to the historical question at issue, but also drawn from other historical problems as well as from the contemporary world situation. In a sense nothing said is really new: that would be impossible by now – but there are shifts in the weight of evidence and belief that will influence subsequent studies, particularly when the implications fit in with other writings. Thus the points in Snooks and in Jackson, suggesting that the Industrial Revolution was more gradual than some used to believe, and, in Snooks, that there had been a long period of economic growth in preceding centuries, whether it was slow and gradual or the net outcome of several wave-like movements, are clearly now, due in no small measure to their work as well as that of others, part of today's standard version. Economic growth does not accelerate very sharply, as many less developed nations have found out recently, and a long introduction period is needed, particularly in the absence of extreme government direction. Nicholas and Oxley's chapter serves to remind us of the somewhat ambiguous nature of economic change as it affects people, male and female, and the always less than clear-cut nature of any social outcome. The arguments in Wrigley's chapter fit in quite well with many of the current writings that seem to see only a limited future for economic growth (as well as a rather limited past). These are all familiar themes that will no doubt recur, though given the sometimes wave-like nature of ideas, perhaps only when next we revisit the Industrial Revolution.

NOTES

1 NEW PERSPECTIVES ON THE INDUSTRIAL REVOLUTION

1 'Technological paradigm shift' is defined in Snooks, *Total Economy*, pp.138–9 and 274.
2 Mokyr (ed.) *Industrial Revolution*. The long chapters by Joel Mokyr, David Landes, and Knick Harley are useful evaluative surveys of the existing literature.
3 Recent work on what I have called the 'new economic revolution' includes Goldin, *The Gender Gap*, and Snooks, *Total Economy*.
4 See Mokyr, 'Introduction'.
5 See Toynbee, *Industrial Revolution*; Mantoux, *Industrial Revolution*; and Ashton, *Industrial Revolution*.
6 Snooks, *Economics without Time*, ch. 3.
7 Deane, *Industrial Revolution*, p. viii. The quantitative outline for this analysis was provided by Deane and Cole, *British Economic Growth*.
8 Rostow, *Stages*, ch. 4. The 'take-off' concept was 'ill-fated' because virtually no evidence could be found to verify Rostow's technical definition (a rise in the investment/GDP ratio from 5 per cent to 10 per cent in a relatively short period of time – in Britain from 1783 to 1802).
9 Deane, *Industrial Revolution*, p. 11.
10 The following quotes are from Mokyr, 'Introduction', pp. 3–4; Landes, 'Fable', pp. 156 and 170; Harley, 'Industrial Revolution', p. 172.
11 Brown and Hopkins, 'Seven centuries'.
12 Snooks, *Economics without Time*, ch. 3.
13 Deane, *Industrial Revolution*, p. 12.
14 For a discussion of the shortrun lagged relationship between population and living standards (Malthus's 'oscillations') see Malthus, *Population*, pp. 77–8; and Ricardo, *Principles*, ch. 32.
15 For an analysis of economic rationality in the Middle Ages see Snooks, *Economics without Time*, ch. 6; McCloskey, 'English open fields'; and McCloskey and Nash, 'Corn at interest'.
16 Lee, 'Pre-industrial England'; and Lee, 'Population history'.
17 Hatcher, *Plague, Population*.

18 Harley, 'Industrial Revolution', p. 209.
19 Harley, 'Industrial Revolution', pp. 171–3.
20 See, for example, Mokyr, 'Introduction', pp. 30–2.
21 Levine, *Reproducing Families*, p. 97; and Coleman, 'Proto-industrialisation', p. 443.
22 Nef's *British Coal* also draws attention to the early use of fossil fuel.
23 Deane and Cole, *British Economic Growth*, p. 7.
24 Cipolla, *European Society*, p. 304. For more recent revisions (50 to 575 thousand people) see Bairoch, *et al.*, *European Cities*, p. 33.
25 Mantoux, *Industrial Revolution*; and Nef, 'Progress of technology'.
26 Landes, *Prometheus*, pp. 5, 7.
27 Persson, *Pre-industrial Economic Growth*. To do so he uses a very simple model based upon the assumption of a precise and stable relationship between agricultural productivity (his proxy for GDP per capita) and urbanization. This simple model depends, unrealistically, on a large number of strong assumptions. See Snooks, *Economics without Time*, pp. 297–8.
28 Thompson, *English Working Class*; Hobsbawm, 'Standard of living'; Ashton, *Industrial Revolution*; and Hartwell, *Economic Growth*.
29 Defined in Snooks, *Total Economy*, pp. 25 and 270.
30 For a summary see Mokyr, 'Introduction', p. 122; and for details see Crafts, *British Economic Growth*, p. 95; and Feinstein, 'Capital accumulation', p. 136.
31 Williamson, *Inequality?*, pp. 14, 17. But see Feinstein, 'Williamson curve', for a rejection of Williamson's support of the Kuznets curve in the British Industrial Revolution, on the grounds that inequality did not increase in the early stages and thereafter decrease, but rather remained largely unchanged.
32 Allen, *Enclosure*, pp. 255–6, 296; and Mokyr, 'Introduction', p. 128.
33 See Feinstein, 'Williamson curve'; Jackson, 'Structure of pay'; and Harley, 'Industrial Revolution'.
34 Wrigley and Schofield, *Population*, p. 529.
35 Huck, 'Infant mortality' (unpublished), quoted in Mokyr, 'Introduction', p. 127.
36 Floud, Wachter, and Gregory, *Height, Health, and History*, using problematical data from the Marine Society.
37 For the most searching criticism of Floud, *et al.* so far, see Komlos, 'Biological standard of living'. Also see Nicholas and Steckel, 'Heights and living standards'.
38 Harley, 'Industrial Revolution', pp. 209–10.
39 Mokyr, 'Introduction', p. 61.
40 Hartwell, in 'Was there an Industrial Revolution?' , p. 4, replies: 'There was an Industrial Revolution and it was British'.
41 Mokyr, *Riches*, ch. 3.
42 As suggested by Landes in 'Fable', pp. 162–3.
43 Harley, 'Industrial Revolution', pp. 225–6.
44 An exponent of the random exogenous shock view is R. Lee, in 'Population history'.
45 It is encouraging to see a recent attempt to estimate real GDP and, hence,

growth rates for other European countries since 1500. See Blomme and Van der Wee, 'The Belgian economy'.

46 Snooks, *Economics without Time*, pp. 241–2.
47 For a discussion of technological change during the Middle Ages, see Mokyr, *Riches*, ch. 3.
48 Snooks, 'The dynamic role of the market'.
49 Harvey, *Peasant Land Market*; Snooks, 'The dynamic role of the market'; McCloskey and Nash, 'Corn at interest'.
50 North and Thomas, *Western World*.
51 Mokyr, *Riches*, ch. 3; Cipolla, *European Society*, ch. 6; Langdon, 'Watermills'; and Langdon, *Horses*.
52 Cipolla, *European Society*, pp. 204–14.
53 Cipolla, *European Society*, p. 276. Also see Coleman, *England*, p. 49.
54 Snooks, *Economics without Time*, p. 241; Miller and Hatcher, *Medieval England*, pp.25–6.
55 Hollister, *Medieval Europe*, Part 2. This is an excellent survey of the entire Middle Ages.
56 Coleman, *England*, p. 49.
57 Snooks, *Economics without Time*, pp. 197–202.
58 Luzzatto, *Economic History of Italy*, p. 145.
59 Clay, *Economic Expansion*, vol. I; Phillips, *Medieval Expansion*; and Davis, *English Overseas Trade*.
60 Bridbury, *Economic Growth*, p. 32.
61 Fisher, 'Commercial trends', p. 153.
62 Much of the data in this paragraph is from Cipolla, *European Society*, pp. 276–96.
63 Mokyr, *Riches*, ch. 3.
64 See Platt, *Medieval England*, especially chs 2 and 7; Snooks, *Economics without Time*, pp. 250–2; Cipolla, *European Society*, pp. 96–110; Mokyr, *Riches*, ch. 3.
65 See Snooks, *Economics without Time*, pp. 176–8, and Gregory King's 'Notebook' (ed. Laslett), p. 65 – categories 7 to 18 as percentage of total population before 1988.
66 Life expectancy at birth did not change significantly between hunter–gatherer societies and the early Middle Ages when it was about 25–30 years. See Quale, *Families*, pp. 43 and 136; and Cohen, *Health*, p. 102.
67 Checkland, *Industrial Society*, pp. 329–30.

2 THE CLASSICAL ECONOMISTS, THE STATIONARY STATE, AND THE INDUSTRIAL REVOLUTION

1 Smith, *Wealth of Nations*, vol. I, pp. 98–9.
2 Smith, *Wealth of Nations*, vol. I, p. 102.
3 Smith, *Wealth of Nations*, vol. I, pp. 90–1, 291–2.
4 Smith, *Wealth of Nations*, vol. I, p. 106.
5 Malthus, *Nature and Progress of Rent*.
6 Ricardo, *Principles*, pp. 125–6.

7 Wrigley, 'Malthus on the prospects for the labouring poor'.

8 With the advent of widespread and effective birth control it has become common to expect to see a negative relationship between living standards and fertility.

9 Mill, *Principles of Political Economy*, vol. I, pp. 182, 340–6.

10 Wrigley, *Continuity, Chance and Change*, pp. 18–19.

11 Wrigley, 'Urban growth and agricultural change'.

12 '. . . who are called philosophers or men of speculation'. Smith, *Wealth of Nations*, vol. I, p. 14.

13 Smith, *Wealth of Nations*, vol. II, p. 404.

14 Wrigley, *Continuity, Chance and Change*, pp. 51–2. See also Wrigley, 'Two kinds of capitalism'.

15 Flinn, *British Coal Industry*, tab. 1.2, p. 26; Nef, *British Coal Industry*, vol. I, tab. I, pp. 19–20.

16 Two tons of dry wood when burnt yields about the same amount of heat energy as one ton of coal, and in favourable circumstances the annual yield of timber per acre is approximately two tons, so that it is a simple matter to calculate how much land would have had to be devoted to wood production to produce the equivalent in heat energy to that provided by a given quantity of coal. White and Plaskett, *Biomass as Fuel*, tab. 1, pp. 12 and 125.

17 Scattered evidence provided by Nef suggests that output per man-year in the seventeenth century was in the range 150–200 tons. He believed that productivity increased considerably in the eighteenth century, especially in the north-east, but the data collected by Mitchell suggest a figure of only just over 200 tons per man-year c.1800. Flinn presented a range of estimates and limited data for the late eighteenth and early nineteenth centuries which do little to reduce the uncertainty. Nef, *British Coal Industry*, vol. II, pp. 138–9; Mitchell, *British Historical Statistics*, pp. 247 and 252; Flinn, *British Coal Industry*, pp. 363–5.

18 Controversy has been especially fierce recently over the use of national income accounting methods to try to quantify growth rates. See Hoppit, 'Counting the industrial revolution'; Jackson, 'Rates of industrial growth'; Berg and Hudson, 'Rehabilitating the industrial revolution'; and Crafts and Harley, 'Output growth'.

19 Already in 1798 Malthus had described the possible reasons for the dynamics of such 'oscillations'. Malthus, *Essay on the Principle of Population* (1798), pp. 14–17.

20 Malthus, *Essay on Population* (1826), pp. 110–15.

21 Jevons, *The Coal Question*.

22 The limited extent of forest cover in England was of very long standing. Rackham concluded that '. . . [the] total woodland area of Domesday England (omitting five northern counties but including Flintshire) comes to 4 million acres, 15% of the land area. These figures involve a good deal of guesswork . . . but our guesses have been generous . . . The figure of 15% is unlikely to be far from the truth and is more likely to be an over-estimate than an under-estimate.' Rackham, *Ancient Woodland*, p. 126; also tab. 96, p. 127.

23 See note 16 above.

24 Fisher, *Energy Crises*, tab. A2.2, pp. 160–1.
25 Kindleberger, *Economic Development*, fig. 4.4, p. 70; Cipolla, *Economic History of World Population*, tab. 4, p. 52.
26 De Zeeuw, 'Peat and the Dutch golden age'.
27 Wrigley, 'The growth of population in eighteenth-century England', pp. 122–3.
28 As might be expected there is a substantial disparity between the estimates that have been made of national real income or GNP per head for this period. A full survey would be tedious, but to indicate the scale of possible disagreement, it is of interest to note that Bairoch's work suggests a large difference beween England and other countries in the early nineteenth century. For 1830 he estimated UK real GNP per head as 370 (in 1960 US dollars) with Belgium, the Netherlands, France, Italy, Germany, and the US all in the range 240–275, the Third World as a whole at 183 and the less developed countries of the Third World at 130. Maddison found a less marked contrast between advanced economies, though an even more marked contrast between them and countries as yet largely untouched by change. He estimated levels of real domestic product per head in 1820, at 1965 US factor cost, as 312 for the UK, 254 for France, and 276 for the US, with undeveloped economies at that date very much lower (e.g. Brazil 97, China 118). Bairoch, 'Trends in national income disparities', tab. 1.3, p. 8, and tab. 1.4, p. 10; Maddison, 'Levels of GDP per capita', tab. 2, p. 30.
29 The relevant volumes of the Cambridge *Agrarian History of England and Wales* contain a mass of empirical data bearing on this point. Two recent books which both contain imaginative discussions of the phenomenon and convenient bibliographic lists are Campbell and Overton, *Land, Labour and Livestock*; and Allen, *Enclosure and the Yeoman*.
30 Nef, *British Coal Industry*, vol. I, p. 239.
31 Flinn, *British Coal Industry*, tab. 7.13, pp. 252–3.
32 See, for example, Smith, *Wealth of Nations*, vol. I, pp. 82–8, or Malthus, *Principles of Political Economy*, pp. 195–211.
33 De Zeeuw argues that it was the fact that much peat in Holland was close to sea level and therefore easy to reach by relatively inexpensive canals which made it economically accessible. However, in one district, the Peel, there was abundant peat but it was 30 metres above sea level and 15 metres above the nearby river Maas. Even this modest difference in height made it impossible to exploit effectively until the middle of the nineteenth century. De Zeeuw, 'Peat and the Dutch golden age', pp. 50–6.

3 GREAT WAVES OF ECONOMIC CHANGE: THE INDUSTRIAL REVOLUTION IN HISTORICAL PERSPECTIVE, 1000 TO 2000

1 This chapter is a development of material first presented in my book, *Economics without Time. A Science Blind to the Forces of Historical Change* (London: Macmillan, 1993). I wish to acknowledge the encouragement and constructive criticism of Warren Hollister, Angus Maddison, and Tom Rymes.

2 See Romer, 'Increasing returns'.

3 This was first attempted in Snooks, 'Last millennium'.

4 At least until Snooks and McDonald, *Domesday Economy*.

5 Results from this research were first presented in Snooks, 'Last millennium'.

6 The term 'great waves' was first coined in Snooks, *Economics without Time*.

7 Estimates of national income for the Roman empire can be found in Goldsmith, 'Roman Empire' and Clark, *Economic Progress*. These estimates are based upon far less comprehensive and reliable data than that in Domesday Book.

8 See Kuznets, *Modern Economic Growth*, p. 139; Rostow, *Stages of Economic Growth*, ch. 2; Maddison, *Capitalist Development*, pp. 6–7; Persson, 'Labour productivity'; and Lee, 'Pre-industrial England'. The recent use of terms such as 'intensive' and 'extensive' growth are regrettable because of the inevitable lapse into the ambiguous use of the abbreviated term 'growth'. I will use 'economic growth' to mean, as economists have always meant, changes in real per capita income, and 'economic expansion' to mean increases in real GDP.

9 Persson, *Economic Growth*. But even his estimates for the sub-periods 1000–1700 (0.1–0.24 per cent per annum) and 1500–1700 (0.28–0.34 per cent per annum) are much lower than mine. And, if he had taken into account the negative rate of growth for 1302–1371, and stagnation and very slow growth from 1372–1491, the long-term rate would have approached zero.

10 Lee, 'Pre-industrial England'; and Maddison, *Capitalist Development*, p. 6.

11 Maddison, *Capitalist Development*, pp. 6–7.

12 Brown and Hopkins, *Perspective*, pp. 19 and 62.

13 Gould, *Economic Growth*; Landes, *Prometheus*; Komlos, *Habsburg Monarchy*.

14 Gould, *Economic Growth*, pp. 35–9.

15 Brown and Hopkins, *Perspective*.

16 Komlos, *Habsburg Monarchy*, p. 221.

17 Landes, *Prometheus*, p. 14.

18 Jones, *Growth Recurring*, p. 4.

19 Jones, *Growth Recurring*, p. 38.

20 Jones, 'Recurrent transitions', p. 45.

21 Jones, *Growth Recurring* and 'Recurrent transitions'.

22 Jones, *European Miracle*.

23 Wrigley, *Continuity*, p. 69.

24 Wrigley and Schofield, *Population*.

25 Hatcher, *English Economy*, pp. 68–9; Smith, 'Demographic developments'; and Snooks, *Economics without Time*.

26 Hatcher, *English Economy*, p. 71 (Figure 2); and Lee, 'Pre-industrial England'.

27 I am currently attempting to quantify the nature of economic change on an annual basis by constructing a series of proxies for per capita income.

28 See Snooks, *Economics without Time*, pp. 178–94.

29 Miller and Hatcher, *Medieval England*, pp. 151 and 161.
30 See Snooks and McDonald, *Domesday Economy*, ch. 7; Snooks, 'Rational calculation'; and Snooks, *Economics without Time*, ch. 6.
31 Darby, *Domesday England*, p. 359. Also see Maitland, *Domesday Book*, pp. 401–2.
32 The details of these estimates can be found in Snooks, 'Last millennium'.
33 See Deane, 'Early national income estimates'; and Lindert and Williamson, 'England's social tables'.
34 Crafts, *British Economic Growth*, pp. 14, 17, 65; and Lindert, 'English occupations'.
35 Crafts, *British Economic Growth*, ch. 2.
36 See Stone, 'War end'; Stone, 'Consumers' behaviour'; and Stone, 'Public finance'.
37 The household consumables index is from Phelps Brown and Hopkins, *Perspective* and the wheat prices are from Rogers, *Agriculture and Prices*, Lloyd, 'Medieval England', and Farmer, 'Angevin England'.
38 See Deane and Cole, *British Economic Growth*, p. 7.
39 Jones, *Miracle*; Cipolla, *European Society*; and Mokyr, *Riches*.
40 Postan, *Medieval Economy*; Miller and Hatcher, *Medieval England*; Bolton, *English Economy*; Dyer, *Middle Ages*.
41 See Snooks, *Economics without Time*, ch. 5.
42 Crafts, *British Economic Growth*; Jones, *Agriculture*.
43 Gould, *Economic Growth*, pp. 34–42.
44 This conclusion appears to have important implications for a measure of living standards that has sky-rocketed in popularity in the last few years – the physical characteristics of the population. Average heights may be a reasonable proxy for the changing average consumption of perishables by a population (provided it is adjusted to the changing energy demands of the work environment), but it has less to say about changes in the consumption of services provided by the changing physical environment. This is particularly important during periods when the major cause of an increase in per capita income is the improvement in infrastructure, as it was in England from the eleventh to the eighteenth centuries. In any case, human height is a highly problematical issue as, unlike material living standards, it is not a variable that economic decision-makers attempt to maximize. Indeed decision-makers may be prepared to trade off extra nutrition (and hence extra height) for the consumption of other non-perishable commodities, or even for the sake of fashion, as appears to be the case with the middle classes in affluent societies today (in which case there will be a negative relationship between heights and living standards). Also see Chapter 6 by Stanley Engerman.
45 Landes, *Prometheus*, p. 14.
46 Platt, *Medieval England*, chs 2 and 7.
47 For example, Mokyr, *Riches*.
48 Phillips, *Medieval Expansion*.
49 Snooks and McDonald, *Domesday Economy*; and Snooks, 'Rational calculation'; Snooks, *Economics without Time*, ch. 6; and Snooks, 'The dynamic role of the market'.

50 Kunitz, 'A long story', p. 275, brings this inadequate data together in tabular form.

51 For example, Gould, *Economic Growth*, and more recently Komlos, *Habsburg Monarchy*.

52 Maddison, *Capitalist Development*, p. 7.

53 This is discussed in Snooks, *Economics without Time*, ch. 3.

54 North and Thomas, *Western World*.

55 Jones, 'Transactions costs'.

56 It is not hard to find contemporary examples of different costs of alternative economic and political systems. Eastern Europe has been grinding to a halt since the 1960s (see data in Maddison, 'European growth') under the inertia of economic systems that are unbelievably inefficient in the way resources, goods and services, and income are allocated.

57 See Snooks, 'Rational calculation', and Chapter 6 below.

58 The simulation employed in Figure 3.3 for the period 1086 to 1688 is based upon a number of solid data sets concerning the trend, amplitude, and shape of the fluctuations in real GDP and GDP per capita. Once these key pieces of data are known we can, with reasonable confidence, simulate these macroeconomic variables. The procedure was as follows: (1) Real GDP was simulated for the period 1086 to 1688 and, as we know the population profile, GDP per capita was estimated as a residual. (2) The *trend* for real GDP was based upon the growth rate (0.49% p.a.) in Table 3.3. (3) The *shape* of the GDP curve was based upon the following data: (a) by combining the population series (interpolated between benchmark years) with the growth trend for GDP per capita (which grew by 0.29% p.a.) a damped outline of real GDP was obtained; (b) this outline was fleshed out by: (i) ensuring that the area between the simulated curve and the trend line, both above and below the line, is equalized; (ii) employing detailed historical evidence about the state of the economy from Hatcher, *English Economy*; Postan, *Medieval Economy*; Bolton, *English Economy*; Dyer, *Middle Ages*; Clarkson, *Pre-Industrial Economy*; and (iii) adopting the assumption, discussed in the text, that there is a positive longrun relationship between population and real GDP. (4) The *amplitude* of the GDP per capita curve between 1300 and 1450 was limited to the increase in manorial income, deflated by the price of wheat, using data from Miller, *Ely*; Dyer, *Worcester*; and Gray, 'Incomes from land'.

59 For a summary of life expectancy rates see Quale, *Families*, p. 136, and Cohen, *Health*, p. 102. Also see Laslett, *Family Life*, and Wrigley and Schofield, *Population*.

60 Brown and Hopkins, 'Prices of consumables'.

61 The Winchester estate manors were scattered through the counties of Berkshire, Buckinghamshire, Hampshire, Oxfordshire, Somerset, Surrey and Wiltshire, together with the Isle of Wight. The number of observations on an annual basis is as high as 40. Yields did not begin to increase significantly until after 1500–1600. See Titow, *English Rural Society* and Clark, 'Yields per acre'.

62 The Winchester yields are *average* yields for an estate that was not

marginal. They cannot be used, therefore, as a test of the classical model.

63　Lee, 'Pre-industrial England', p. 606.

64　Hatcher, *English Economy*, pp. 69–70.

65　Hatcher, *English Economy*, pp. 33–4.

66　Abel, *Agricultural Fluctuation*, pp. 45 and 46.

67　Postan, *Medieval Economy*, pp. 275–6; see also p. 40.

68　Abel, *Agricultural Fluctuations*, p. 42.

69　Langdon, 'Water-mills', p. 430, shows that from 1301–50 and 1351–1400 the number of watermills in West Midland fell by 40.3 per cent.

70　Poos, *A Rural Society*, pp. 52 and 211. Curiously, Poos attempts to support the traditional argument ('In general the Essex evidence confirms the traditional picture', p. 212) using only nominal wages. When nominal wages (p. 211) are compared with prices (p. 52) – something that Poos fails to do – it is clear that *real* wages declined by almost one-quarter. The traditional wisdom transcends even hard-won evidence.

71　Data from the Medieval Taxes Project AD 991 to 1500 by Carolyn Fenwick and G.D. Snooks, RSSS, ANU.

72　Schofield, 'Wealth in England'.

73　Hatcher, *English Economy*, p. 33. See also Mokyr, *Riches*, chs 3 and 8.

74　Hatcher, *English Economy*, pp. 31–5, provides indirect evidence of a brief recovery.

75　The above scenario is certainly not consistent with an increase in nominal wages in the Brown–Hopkins index of up to two-thirds between 1347 and the early 1350s, or an increase in real wages of 21 per cent between 1347 and 1349, and 42 per cent between 1347 and 1361. But there are further and more important reasons for rejecting the Brown–Hopkins nominal and real wage rate indexes. Consider what they purport to show. The real wage-rate index shows a marked *increase* during the depressed conditions of the late fourteenth and fifteenth centuries; an even more marked *decrease* during the expansion of the sixteenth century – by which time real wages were below those prior to 1300 – and then a slow recovery through two phases in the early eighteenth and nineteenth centuries, until, finally, by the mid-1880s, the former peak in the 1470s had just been exceeded. Think of it: real wage rates are alleged to be higher in 1477 than they were in the late Victorian period over 400 years later. So much for the impact of technological change and the increase in the capital–labour ratio on labour productivity. It implies that the labour supply curve shifted outwards much more rapidly than the demand curve over those 400 years. Also the dramatic fall in this real wage rate index between 1500 and 1600 contradicts the usual interpretation (by Jones, Maddison, Clarkson, and others) that this period experienced slow growth of per capita income, and also the findings of Wrigley and Schofield that life expectancy rose during this period. Indeed, Wrigley and Schofield expressed puzzlement about the inverse relationship between their life expectancy curve and the Brown–Hopkins real wage index (see Wrigley and Schofield, *Population*, p. 414). My 'great waves' diagram provides a more plausible explanation of life expectancy, not only since 1500 but for the entire millennium since AD1000.

Clearly there is a major problem with the nominal wage data employed by Brown and Hopkins. Throughout much of the Middle Ages labour 'markets' were primitive and very local in nature. They were largely under the control of local squires or major urban employers. Also the data are not wage rates but piece rates and it is impossible to determine how many workers were involved in individual contracts (see Poos, *A Rural Society*, ch. 10). The available wage data for the Middle Ages are completely unreliable and certainly cannot be employed as a proxy for real GDP per capita. In any case there is no reason to suppose that real wages and real non-wage GDP per capita will change in the same way.

76 Clay, *Economic Expansion*, vol. I, p. 126, notes the slow increase in agricultural productivity in the sixteenth century. Also see Clarkson, *Pre-Industrial Economy*, chs 3 to 5.
77 Clay, *Economic Expansion*, p. 141.
78 Mokyr, *Riches*, chs 5 and 10.
79 See Snooks, 'The dynamic role of markets'.

4 WHAT WAS THE RATE OF ECONOMIC GROWTH DURING THE INDUSTRIAL REVOLUTION?

1 Dean and Cole, *British Economic Growth*, ch. 2.
2 Cole and Deane, 'Growth of incomes', p. 10. None the less, Deane and Cole argued that the crucial beginnings of economic growth can be dated from the 1740s.
3 Harley, 'British industrialization'; Crafts, *British Economic Growth*, ch. 2.
4 Preface to the first edition of Deane and Cole, *British Economic Growth*.
5 Harley, 'British industrialization'.
6 Hoffmann, *British Industry*.
7 Crafts, *British Economic Growth*, p. 2.
8 Crafts and Harley, 'Output growth', p. 715.
9 This formulation of Deane and Cole's procedure ignores the adjustments they made to allow for net exports of agricultural products. The account of Crafts's procedure below also ignores the adjustment he made on this account because this is a minor complication in the context of the present discussion. Accuracy of detail is here sacrificed for the sake of a clearer view of the fundamentals.
10 Crafts, *British Economic Growth*, pp. 35, 37; Deane and Cole, *British Economic Growth*, pp. 6, 78.
11 Crafts, *British Economic Growth*, pp. 40–1; Deane and Cole, *British Economic Growth*, p. 91.
12 Crafts, *British Economic Growth*, p. 45; Lindert and Williamson, 'Social tables'.
13 Crafts, *British Economic Growth*, pp. 28–9.
14 Pollard, 'Coal production'; Riden, 'Iron industry'; Feinstein, 'Capital formation'.
15 Deane, 'Woollen industry'; Deane and Cole, *British Economic Growth*, chs 2, 6; Mitchell and Deane, *Abstract*.

16 Crafts, *British Economic Growth*, p. 35.
17 Jackson, 'Growth and deceleration'.
18 Crafts, *British Economic Growth*, p. 41.
19 See the comparison of the Hoffmann index (*British Industry*, table 54) with the CLM index (Crafts, Leybourne, and Mills, 'Trends and cycles', p. 58) in Jackson, 'Industrial growth', pp. 10–11.
20 Jackson, 'Government expenditure', pp. 226–30.
21 The same reservations, of course, apply to my calculations of agricultural growth (Jackson, 'Growth and deceleration').
22 Crafts, *British Economic Growth*, ch. 4.
23 This ignores the fact that Crafts's estimate of R in equation 9 is not wholly independent of the remainder of his estimates.
24 Note that P, e, and n are still assumed to have been accurate. To allow P to vary would complicate the example without affecting the basic point. The calculations are less sensitive to variations in e and n than might appear so long as the absolute value of e is assumed to be close to the value of n (that is, so long as the cross elasticity of demand is assumed to have been small).
25 Crafts, 'Reappraisal'.
26 Deane and Cole, *British Economic Growth*, p. 282.
27 Deane and Cole, *British Economic Growth*, pp. 166, 170, 282; Mitchell and Deane, *Abstract*, p. 471. Because the Rousseaux indexes begin in 1800, the 1801 estimates have been deflated by indexes averaged over the five years 1800 to 1804. Nine-year centred averages have been used for 1831. This produced estimates of gross national product in 1865/85 prices of £139 million in 1801 and £312 million in 1831, compared with Deane and Cole's estimates of £138 and £312 million.
28 Crafts, *British Economic Growth*, p. 41.
29 O'Brien, 'Home market', pp. 787–90; Mitchell and Deane, *Abstract*, pp. 495, 499; Beveridge, *Prices and Wages*, pp. 425–6, 429.
30 Crafts, *British Economic Growth*, p. 41.
31 Jackson, 'Growth and deceleration', pp. 343–9.
32 Feinstein, 'Capital formation', p. 42.
33 Crafts (*British Economic Growth*, p. 29) derived his canal estimate from the graphs in Hawke, *Railways and Economic Growth*, p. 81, and his estimate for stage travel from parliamentary papers for 1857.
34 Williamson, 'Structure of pay'; Deane and Cole, *British Economic Growth*, p. 143.
35 Deane and Cole, *British Economic Growth*, p. 143.
36 Crafts estimated that labour productivity in government and the professions rose at 1.37 per cent a year compared with the 1.32 per cent that is implicit in Deane and Cole's estimates.
37 Feinstein, 'National statistics', p. 448; Crafts and Harley, 'Output growth', p. 715.
38 The growth rate for trade and transport combined turns out to be a U-shaped function of the estimated growth in transport output. The function reaches a minumum value when transport growth is 2.36 per cent a year. Annual growth in trade and transport combined is then only 0.02 percentage points below the growth rate produced by the figure for

transport growth which Crafts uses (3.02 per cent). Transport growth below 1.76 per cent or above 3.02 per cent a year implies growth in trade and transport combined which is somewhat higher than Crafts's estimate.

39 Crafts, 'Reappraisal', p. 180.
40 Jackson, 'Industrial growth'.
41 Crafts, 'Reappraisal', p. 180.
42 Crafts, *British Economic Growth*, pp. 17–34.
43 Crafts, 'Reappraisal', pp. 182–3.
44 Crafts, *British Economic Growth*, pp. 29, 36.
45 The employment figures are taken from Deane and Cole, *British Economic Growth*, p.143.
46 This is not to say that the evidence Crafts used is reliable. For a discussion of the deficiencies in Williamson's estimates of the structure of pay, see Feinstein, 'Williamson curve'; Jackson, 'Structure of pay'.
47 Crafts and Harley, 'Output growth', p. 717.
48 Deane and Cole, *British Economic Growth*, pp. xvii, 278.
49 Crafts, 'Reappraisal', p. 184.

5 THE INDUSTRIAL REVOLUTION AND THE GENESIS OF THE MALE BREADWINNER

1 Thomas, 'Women and capitalism', p. 545.
2 Anon., 'Employment of females'; Greg, *Literary and Social Judgements*; Kaye, 'Employment of women'; Oliphant, 'The condition of women'; Parkes, *Essays on Women's Work*; UK, 'Report on the Employment of Children', Smith Baker, 'Social results'; Stanton, *The Woman Question*; Wright, 'Employment of women in factories'. Also see references in Humphries, 'Enclosures, common rights, and women'; Jordan, 'Exclusion of women'; Thomas, 'Women and capitalism'.
3 For example, Hobsbawm, *Labouring Men*; Thompson, *Making of the English Working Class*. For some critiques see Alexander, Davin and Hostettler, 'Labouring women'; Scott, *Gender* (especially Chapter 4); Seccombe, 'Patriarchy stabilized'.
4 Ehrenreich and English, *For Her Own Good*.
5 Early factory textile workers were often female, as their part of the production process was the first drawn into mechanized production, generating much concern among observers like Frederick Engels, *Condition of the Working Class*. Mining, for example, still employed families in some areas; see Humphries, 'Protective legislation'.
6 Tilly and Scott, *Women, Work and Family*.
7 Berg, *Age of Manufactures*; McBride, *Domestic Revolution*; Malcolmson, *English Laundresses*.
8 Jordan, 'Exclusion of women'.
9 Davidoff and Hall, *Family Fortunes*.
10 Burman, *Fit Work for Women*; Humphries, '"Most free from objection"'; Richards, 'Women in the British economy'; Roberts, 'Sickles and scythes'; Snell, 'Agricultural seasonal unemployment'. For a very interesting recent discussion of the role of ideology in determining

women's work, see Jordan, 'Exclusion of women'.

11 Alexander, 'Women's work'; Snell, *Annals*.
12 Humphries, 'Enclosures, common rights, and women'.
13 Holley, 'Two family economies'; Land, 'Family wage'; Seccombe, 'Patriarchy stabilized'.
14 Pinchbeck, *Women Workers*, p. 311.
15 Pinchbeck and Hewitt, *Children in English Society*, quoted in McKendrick, 'Home demand', p. 161.
16 Pinchbeck, *Women Workers*, p. 313.
17 Shorter, *Making the Modern Family*; Shorter, 'Women's work'. See Thomas, 'Women and capitalism', p. 537.
18 Goode, *World Revolution*; Fox-Genovese, 'Placing women's history', pp. 21–2; Shorter, *Women's Bodies*.
19 McKendrick, 'Home demand', p. 185.
20 Young and Wilmott, *Symmetrical Family*.
21 Thomas, 'Women and capitalism', p. 545.
22 Anderson, *Western Family*, p. 51; Pahl, *Divisions of Labour*, pp. 20–1.
23 Sen and Sengupta, 'Malnutrition', p. 863.
24 Behrman, 'Intrahousehold allocation'.
25 Sen and Sengupta, 'Malnutrition', p. 863.
26 Sen, '100 million missing', pp. 62–4; Pitt, *et al.*, 'Productivity, health and inequality', pp. 1139–41.
27 Sen and Sengupta, 'Malnutrition', p. 863.
28 Eveleth and Tanner, *Worldwide Variation*; Fogel, *et al.*, 'Secular changes'.
29 Steckel, 'Height and income'.
30 Scrimshaw, 'Interactions'.
31 Floud, Wachter and Gregory, *Height, Health and History*; Fogel, *et al.*, 'Secular changes'; Steckel, 'Heights and income'; Komlos, *Nutrition and Economic Development*; Nicholas and Oxley, 'Living standards'.
32 Jarque-Bera tests which compare the first four moments of the sample distributions with the normal distribution were used to assess the normality properties of the height distributions after rounding all female heights to the half inch. See Nicholas and Oxley, 'Living standards' and Nicholas and Steckel, 'Heights and living standards'.
33 Fogel, *et al.*, 'Secular changes'; Steckel, 'Stature and living standards in the US'.
34 The quality of the male data has been assessed in Nicholas and Steckel, 'Heights and living standards'; Nicholas and Shergold, 'Intercounty labour mobility'; and Nicholas and Shergold, 'Internal migration'; and found to be broadly representative of the male working population.
35 86 per cent of convicts' skills were from the following 12 jobs (in descending order of significance): housemaid, allwork, kitchenmaid, nursemaid, cook, laundress, dairymaid, needlewoman, country servant, laundrymaid, washerwoman, and children's maid.
36 Armstrong, 'Use of information about occupation'.
37 Mokyr and O'Grada, 'Emigration and poverty', p. 379.
38 Beattie, *Crime and the Courts*; Emsley, *Crime and Society*; Jones, *Crime, Protest, Community*; Philips, *Crime and Authority*; Rudé, *Criminal and Victim*.

39 Oxley, 'Women transported'.
40 Eveleth and Tanner, *Worldwide Variations*, p. 1.
41 Burnett, *Plenty and Want*; Shammas, 'English diet'.
42 Burnett, *Plenty and Want*, p. 22.
43 Schofield, 'Dimensions of illiteracy'; Schofield, 'Age-specific mobility', pp. 265–6.
44 Snell, 'Agricultural seasonal unemployment'; Roberts, 'Sickles and scythes'.
45 Humphries, '"Bread and a pennyworth of treacle"', p. 471.
46 Thomas, 'Women and capitalism', p. 537.
47 Land, 'Family wage', pp. 58–9.

SELECT BIBLIOGRAPHY

Abel, W., *Agricultural Fluctuations in Europe: From the Thirteenth to the Twentieth Centuries*, London, Methuen, 1980.

Alexander, S., 'Women's work in nineteenth century London: a study of the years 1820–50', in J. Mitchell and A. Oakley (eds), *The Rights and Wrongs of Women*, Harmondsworth, Penguin, 1976, pp. 59–111.

Alexander, S., Davin, A. and Hostettler, E., 'Labouring women: a reply to Eric Hobsbawm', *History Workshop*, 8, 1979, pp. 174–82.

Allen, R.C., *Enclosure and the Yeoman*, Oxford, Clarendon Press, 1992.

Anderson, M., *Approaches to the History of the Western Family 1500–1914*, London, Macmillan, 1980.

anon., 'Employment of females', *Transactions of the National Association for the Promotion of Social Science*, 12, 1868.

Armstrong, W.A., 'The use of information about occupation', in E.A. Wrigley (ed.), *Nineteenth-Century Society: Essays in the Use of Quantitative Methods for the Study of Social Data*, Cambridge, Cambridge University Press, 1972, pp. 191–310.

Ashton, T.S., *The Industrial Revolution, 1760–1830*, Oxford, Oxford University Press, 1948.

Babbage, Charles, *On the Economy of Machinery and Manufactures*, Philadelphia, Carey & Lea, 1832.

Bairoch, P., 'The main trends in national economic disparities since the industrial revolution', in P. Bairoch and M. Lévy-Leboyer (eds), *Disparities in Economic Development since the Industrial Revolution*, London, Macmillan, 1981, pp. 3–17.

Bairoch, P., Batou, J. Chèvre, P., *The Population of European Cities, 800–1850: Data Bank and Short Summary of Results*, Geneva, Droz, 1988.

Beattie, J.M., 'Criminality of women in eighteenth-century England', *Journal of Social History*, 8, 1975, pp. 80–116.

Beattie, J.M., *Crime and the Courts in England, 1660–1800*, Princeton, NJ, Princeton University Press, 1986.

Behrman, J., 'Intrahousehold allocation of nutrients in rural India: Are boys favoured? Do parents exhibit inequality aversion?', *Oxford Economic Papers*, 40, 1988, pp. 32–54.

Berg, M., *The Age of Manufactures: Industry, Innovation and Work in Britain, 1700–1820*, Oxford, Blackwell in association with Fontana, 1985.

Berg, M. and Hudson, P., 'Rehabilitating the industrial revolution', *Economic History Review*, 45, 1992, pp. 24–50.

Beveridge, W., *Prices and Wages in England from the Twelfth to the Nineteenth Century*, London, Longmans Green, 1939.

Blomme, J. and Van der Wee, H., 'The Belgian economy in the very long run, 1500–1812', in *Proceedings of the Eleventh International Economic History Conference, Session B (13), Milan, 1994*.

Bolton, J.L., *The Medieval English Economy, 1150–1500*, London, Kent, 1980.

Bridbury, A.R., *Economic Growth: England in the Later Middle Ages*, London, Allen & Unwin, 1962.

Brown, H.P. and Hopkins, S.V. (eds), *A Perspective of Wages and Prices*, London & New York, Methuen, 1981.

Brown, H.P. and Hopkins, S.V., 'Seven centuries of the prices of consumables, compared with builders' wage-rates', in H.P. Brown and S.V. Hopkins (eds), *A Perspective of Wages and Prices*, London & New York, Methuen, 1981, pp. 13–59.

Burman, S. (ed.), *Fit Work for Women*, London, Croom Helm, and Canberra, Australian National University Press, 1979.

Burnett, J., *Plenty and Want: A Social History of Diet in England from 1815 to the Present Day*, London, Nelson, 1966.

Campbell, B.M.S. and Overton, M. (eds), *Land, Labour and Livestock: Historical Studies in European Agricultural Productivity*, Manchester, Manchester University Press, 1991.

Checkland, S.G., *The Rise of Industrial Society in England, 1815–1885*, London, Longmans, 1964.

Cipolla, C.M., *The Economic History of World Population*, Harmondsworth, Penguin, 1962.

Cipolla, C.M., *Before the Industrial Revolution: European Society and Economy, 1000–1700*, London, Methuen, 1976.

Clark, A., *Working Life of Women in the Seventeenth Century*, London, Routledge & Kegan Paul, 1919.

Clark, C.G., *The Conditions of Economic Progress*, London, Macmillan, 1940.

Clark, G., 'Yields per acre in English agriculture, 1250–1860: evidence from labour inputs', *Economic History Review*, 2nd ser., 44, August 1991, pp. 445–60.

Clarkson, L.A., *The Pre-Industrial Economy in England, 1500–1750*, London, Batsford, 1971.

Clay, C.G.A., *Economic Expansion and Social Change: England 1500–1700*, 2 vols, Cambridge, Cambridge University Press, 1984.

Cohen, M.N., *Health and the Rise of Civilisation*, New Haven & London, Yale University Press, 1989.

Cole, W.A. and Deane, P., 'The growth of national incomes', in H.J. Habakkuk and M.M. Postan (eds), *The Cambridge Economic History of Europe*, vol. 6, Cambridge, Cambridge University Press, 1965, pp. 1–59.

Coleman, D.C., *The Economy of England, 1450–1750*, London, Oxford University Press, 1977.

Coleman, D.C., 'Proto-industrialization: a concept too many', *Economic History Review*, 2nd ser., 36, 1983, pp. 435–48.

Convict Indents, 1817–1840, Archives Office of New South Wales, Sydney.

Crafts, N.F.R., 'National income estimates and the British standard of living debate: a reappraisal of 1801–1831', *Explorations in Economic History*, 17, 1980, pp. 176–88.

Crafts, N.F.R., *British Economic Growth during the Industrial Revolution*, Oxford, Clarendon Press, 1985.

Crafts, N.F.R. and Harley, C.K., 'Output growth and the British industrial revolution: a restatement of the Crafts–Harley view', *Economic History Review*, 45, 1992, pp. 703–30.

Crafts, N.F.R., Leybourne, S.J. and Mills, T.C., 'Trends and cycles in British industrial production, 1700–1913', *Journal of the Royal Statistical Society*, ser. A, 152, 1989, pp. 43–60.

Darby, H.C., *Domesday England*, Cambridge, Cambridge University Press, 1979.

Davidoff, L. and Hall, C., *Family Fortunes: Men and Women of the English Middle Class, 1780–1850*, London, Hutchinson, 1987.

Davis, R., *English Overseas Trade, 1500–1700*, London, Macmillan, 1973.

De Zeeuw, J.W., 'Peat and the Dutch golden age: the historical meaning of energy attainability', *A.A.G. Bijdragen*, 21, 1978, pp. 3–31.

Deane, P., 'The implications of early national income estimates for the measurement of long-term economic growth in the United Kingdom', *Economic Development and Cultural Change*, 4, 1955, pp. 3–38.

Deane, P., 'The output of the British woollen industry in the eighteenth century', *Journal of Economic History*, 17, 1957, pp. 207–23.

Deane, P. and Cole, W.A., *British Economic Growth, 1688–1959: Trends and Structure*, Cambridge, Cambridge University Press, 1962; 2nd edn, 1967.

Deane, P., *The First Industrial Revolution*, Cambridge, Cambridge University Press, 1965.

Dyer, C., *Lords and Peasants in a Changing Society: The Estates of the Bishopric of Worcester, 680–1540*, Cambridge, Cambridge University Press, 1980.

Dyer, C., *Standards of Living in the Later Middle Ages: Social Change in England, 1200–1520*, Cambridge & New York, Cambridge University Press, 1989.

Ehrenreich, B. and English, D., *For Her Own Good: 50 Years of the Experts' Advice to Women*, London, Pluto Press, 1979.

Eliot, T.S., 'East Coker', *Collected Poems 1902–62*, London, Faber & Faber, 1963, pp. 196–204.

Emsley, C., *Crime and Society in England, 1750–1900*, London & New York, Longman, 1987.

Engels, F., *The Condition of the Working Class in England* (translated and edited by W.O. Henderson and W.H. Chaloner), Oxford, Blackwell, 1971.

Eveleth, P.B. and Tanner, J.M., *Worldwide Variation in Human Growth*, Cambridge & New York, Cambridge University Press, 1976.

Farmer, D.L., 'Some price fluctuations in Angevin England', *Economic History Review*, 2nd ser., 9, August 1956, pp. 34–43.

Feinstein, C.H., 'Capital formation in Great Britain', in P. Mathias and M.M. Postan (eds), *The Cambridge Economic History of Europe*, vol. 7, Cambridge, Cambridge University Press, 1978, pp. 28–96.

Feinstein, C.H., 'Capital accumulation and the Industrial Revolution', in R. Floud and D.N. McCloskey (eds), *The Economic History of Britain Since 1700*, vol. 1, Cambridge, Cambridge University Press, 1981, pp. 128–42.

Feinstein, C.H., 'National statistics, 1760–1820', in C.H. Feinstein and S. Pollard (eds), *Studies in Capital Formation in the United Kingdom*, Oxford, Clarendon Press, 1988, pp. 258–401.

Feinstein, C.H., 'The rise and fall of the Williamson curve', *Journal of Economic History*, 48, 1988, pp. 699–729.

Finberg, H.P.R., *et al.* (eds), *The Agrarian History of England and Wales*, Cambridge, Cambridge University Press, 1967–.

Fisher, F.J., 'Commercial trends and policy in sixteenth-century England', in E.M. Carus-Wilson (ed.), *Essays in Economic History: Reprints*, 3 vols, London, E. Arnold, 1954–1962.

Fisher, J.C., *Energy Crises in Perspective*, New York, Wiley, 1974.

Flinn, M.W., *The History of the British Coal Industry*, vol. 2: *1700–1830: The Industrial Revolution*, Oxford, Clarendon Press, 1984.

Floud, R., Wachter, K. and Gregory, A.S., *Height, Health and History: Nutritional Status in the United Kingdom, 1750–1980*, Cambridge, Cambridge University Press, 1990.

Fogel, R.W., *Railroads and American Economic Growth: Essays in Econometric History*, Baltimore, MD, Johns Hopkins University Press, 1964.

Fogel, R.W., Engerman, S., Floud, R., Steckel, R., Trussell, J., Wachter, K., Murgo, R., Sokoloff, K. and Villaflor, G., 'Secular changes in American and British stature and nutrition', *Journal of Interdisciplinary History*, 14, 1983, pp. 445–81.

Fox-Genovese, E., 'Placing women's history in history', *New Left Review*, 133, 1982, pp.5–29.

Goldin, C., *Understanding the Gender Gap: An Economic History of American Women*, New York, Oxford University Press, 1990.

Goldsmith, R.W., 'An estimate of the size and structure of the national product of the early Roman Empire', *Review of Income and Wealth*, Series 30, September 1984, pp.263–88.

Goode, W., *World Revolution and Family Patterns*, New York, Free Press of Glencoe, 1963.

Gould, J.D., *Economic Growth in History: Survey and Analysis*, London, Methuen, 1972.

Gray, H.L., 'Incomes from land in England in 1436', *English Historical Review*, 49, October 1934, pp. 607–39.

Greg, W.R., *Literary and Social Judgements*, London, Trubner, 1868.

Habakkuk, H.J., *Population Growth and Economic Development since 1750*, Leicester, Leicester University Press, 1971.

Harley, C.K., 'British industrialization before 1841: evidence of slower growth during the Industrial Revolution', *Journal of Economic History*, 42, 1982, pp. 267–89.

Harley, C.K., 'Reassessing the Industrial Revolution: a macro view', in J. Mokyr (ed.), *The British Industrial Revolution: An Economic Perspective*, Boulder, San Francisco and Oxford, Westview Press, 1993, pp. 171–226.

Hartwell, R.M., *The Industrial Revolution and Economic Growth*, London, Methuen, 1971.

Hartwell, R.M., 'Was there an Industrial Revolution?' *Social Science History*, 14, 1990, pp. 567–76.

Harvey, P.D.A. (ed.), *The Peasant Land Market in Medieval England*, Oxford, Clarendon Press; New York, Oxford University Press, 1984.

Hatcher, J., *Plague, Population, and the English Economy, 1348–1530*, London, Macmillan, 1977.

Hawke, G.R., *Railways and Economic Growth in England and Wales 1840–1870*, Oxford, Clarendon Press, 1970.

Hobsbawm, E.J., *Labouring Men: Studies in the History of Labour*, London, Weidenfeld & Nicolson, 1964.

Hobsbawm, E.J., 'The standard of living debate', in A.J. Taylor (ed.), *The Standard of Living in Britain in the Industrial Revolution*, London, Methuen, 1975, pp. 58–92.

Hoffmann, W.G., *British Industry 1700–1850*, Oxford, Blackwell, 1955.

Holley, J.C., 'The two family economies of industrialism: factory workers in Victorian Scotland', *Journal of Family History*, 6, 1981, pp. 57–69.

Hollister, C. Warren, *Medieval Europe: A short history*, New York, Alfred A. Knopf, 1982.

Hoppit, J., 'Counting the industrial revolution', *Economic History Review*, 2nd ser., 43, 1990, pp. 173–93.

Huck, P.F., Infant mortality and the standard of living during the Industrial Revolution, unpublished PhD dissertation, Northwestern University, 1992.

Humphries, J., 'Protective legislation, the capitalist state, and working class men: the case of the 1842 Mines Regulation Act', *Feminist Review*, 7, 1981, pp. 1–33.

Humphries, J., '". . . The most free from objection . . .": The sexual division of labour and women's work in nineteenth-century England', *Journal of Economic History*, 47, 1987, pp. 929–49.

Humphries, J., 'Enclosures, common rights and women: the proletarianization of families in the late eighteenth and early nineteenth centuries', *Journal of Economic History*, 50, 1990, pp. 17–42.

Humphries, J., '"Bread and a pennyworth of treacle": excess female mortality in England in the 1840s', *Cambridge Journal of Economics*, 15, December 1991, pp. 451–73.

Jackson, R.V., 'Growth and deceleration in English agriculture, 1660–1790', *Economic History Review*, 2nd ser., 38, 1985, pp. 333–51.

Jackson, R.V., 'The structure of pay in nineteenth-century Britain', *Economic History Review*, 2nd ser., 40, 1987, pp. 561–70.

Jackson, R.V., 'Government expenditure and British economic growth in the eighteenth century: some problems of measurement', *Economic History Review*, 2nd ser., 43, 1990, pp. 217–35.

Jackson, R.V., 'Rates of industrial growth during the Industrial Revolution', *Economic History Review*, 45, 1992, pp. 1–23.

Jevons, H.S., *The British Coal Trade*, London, Kegan Paul Trench Trubner, 1915.

Jevons, W.S., *The Coal Question: An Inquiry Concerning the Progress of the Nation and the Probable Exhaustion of Our Coal Mines*, London, Macmillan, 1865.

Jones, D.J.V., *Crime, Protest, Community and Police in Nineteenth-Century Britain*, London, David Jones; Boston, Routledge & Kegan Paul 1982.

Jones, E.L., *Agriculture and Economic Growth in England, 1650–1815*, London, Methuen, 1967.

Jones, E.L., *The European Miracle: Environments, Economies and Geopolitics in the History of Europe and Asia*, Cambridge, Cambridge University Press, 1981.

Jones, E.L., *Growth Recurring: Economic Change in World History*, Oxford, Clarendon Press, 1988.

Jones, E.L., 'Recurrent transitions to *intensive* growth', in J. Goudsblom *et al.* (eds), *Human History and Social Progress*, Exeter, University of Exeter Press, 1989, pp. 46–62.

Jones, S.R.H., 'Transactions costs, institutional change and the emergence of a market economy in later Anglo-Saxon England', *Economic History Review*, 2nd ser., 46 November 1993, pp. 658–78.

Jordan, E., 'The exclusion of women from industry in nineteenth-century Britain', *Comparative Studies in Social History*, 31, 1989, pp. 273–96.

Kaye, J.W., 'The employment of women', *North British Review*, 26, 1857.

Kindleberger, C.P., *Economic Development*, 2nd edn, New York, 1965.

King, Gregory, *Two Tracts by Gregory King* (ed. G.E. Barnett), Baltimore, The Johns Hopkins Press, 1936.

King, Gregory, 'The L.C.C. Burns journal: a manuscript notebook containing workings for several projected works (composed c. 1695–1700)', in *The Earliest Classics: John Braunt and Gregory King* (with an introduction by Peter Laslett), Farnborough, Hants, Gregg, 1973.

Komlos, J., *Nutrition and Economic Development in the Eighteenth Century Habsburg Monarchy: An Anthropometric History*, Princeton, NJ, Princeton University Press, 1989.

Komlos, J., *Nutrition and Economic Development in the Eighteenth Century Habsburg Monarchy: An Anthropometric History*, Princeton, NJ, Princeton University Press, 1989.

Komlos, J., 'The secular trend in the biological standard of living in the UK, 1730–1860', *Economic History Review*, 2nd ser., 46, February 1993, pp. 115–44.

Kunitz, S.J., 'Making a long story short: a note on men's height and mortality in England from the first through the nineteenth centuries', *Medical History*, 31, 1987, pp. 269–80.

Kuznets, S., *Modern Economic Growth: Rate, Structure, and Spread*, New Haven, Yale University Press, 1966.

Land, H., 'The family wage', *Feminist Review*, 6, 1980, pp. 55–77.

Landes, D.S., *The Unbound Prometheus: Technological Changes and Industrial Development in Western Europe from 1750 to the Present*, London, Cambridge University Press, 1969.

Landes, D.S., 'The fable of the dead horse; or, the Industrial Revolution revisited', in J. Mokyr (ed.), *The British Industrial Revolution: An Economic Perspective*, Boulder, San Francisco and Oxford, Westview Press, 1993, pp. 132–70.

Langdon, J., *Horses, Oxen, and Technological Innovation: The Use of Draught Animals in English Farming from 1066 to 1500*, Cambridge & New York, Cambridge University Press, 1986.

Langdon, J., 'Water-mills and windmills in the west Midlands, 1086–1500', *Economic History Review*, 2nd ser., 44, August 1991, pp. 424–44.

Laslett, P., *Family Life and Illicit Love in Earlier Generations*, Cambridge, Cambridge University Press, 1977.

Lee, R., 'Population in pre-industrial England: an econometric analysis', *Quarterly Journal of Economics*, 87, 1973, pp. 581–607.

Lee, R., 'Accidental and systematic change in population history: homeostasis in a stochastic setting', *Explorations in Economic History*, vol. 30, no. 1, January 1993, pp. 1–30.

Levine, D., *Reproducing Families: The Political Economy of English Population History*, Cambridge, Cambridge University Press, 1987.

Lindert, P.H., 'English occupations: 1670–1811', *Journal of Economic History*, 40, 1980, pp. 685–712.

Lindert, P.H. and Williamson, J.G., 'Revising England's social tables, 1688–1812', *Explorations in Economic History*, 19, 1982, pp. 385–408.

Lindert, P.H. and Williamson, J.G., 'Revising England's social tables 1688–1812', *Explorations in Economic History*, 20, 1982, pp. 94–109.

Lloyd, T.H., 'The movement of wool prices in medieval England', *Economic History Review*, Supplement No. 6, 1973.

Luzzatto, G., *An Economic History of Italy from the Fall of the Roman Empire to the Beginning of the Sixteenth Century*, London, Routledge & Kegan Paul, 1961.

McBride, T., *The Domestic Revolution: The Modernisation of Household Service in England and France 1820–1920*, New York, Holmes & Meier, 1976.

McCloskey, D.N., 'English open fields as behaviour towards risk', *Research in Economic History*, 1, 1976, pp. 124–70.

McCloskey, D.N. and Nash, J., 'Corn at interest: the cost of grain storage in medieval England', *American Economic Review*, 24, March 1984, pp. 174–87.

McKendrick, N., 'Home demand and economic growth: a new view of the role of women and children in the industrial revolution', in N. McKendrick (ed.), *Historical Perspectives, Studies in English Thought and Society*, London, Europa, 1974, pp. 152–210.

Maddison, A., *Phases of Capitalist Development*, New York, Oxford University Press, 1982.

Maddison, A., 'A comparison of GDP per capita in developed and developing countries, 1700–1980', *Journal of Economic History*, 43, 1983, pp. 27–41.

Maddison, A., Measuring European growth: the core and the periphery, paper presented to the Tenth International Conference in Economic History, Leuven, Belgium, 1990.

Maitland, F.W., *Domesday Book and Beyond: Three Essays in the Early History of England*, Cambridge, Cambridge University Press, 1921.

Malcolmson, P.E., *English Laundresses: A Social History, 1850–1930*, Urbana, University of Illinois Press, 1986.

Malthus, T.R., *An Essay on the Principle of Population as it Affects the Future Improvement of Society* (London, 1798), in E.A. Wrigley and D. Souden (eds), *The Works of Thomas Robert Malthus*, vol. 1, London, W. Pickering, 1986.

Malthus, T.R., *An Inquiry into the Nature and Progress of Rent, and the Principles by which it is Regulated* (London, 1815), in E.A. Wrigley and D. Souden (eds), *The Works of Thomas Robert Malthus*, vol. 7, London, W. Pickering, 1986, pp. 111–45.

Malthus, T.R., *Principles of Political Economy Considered with a View to their Practical Application* (2nd edn, London, 1836), in E.A. Wrigley and D. Souden (eds), *The Works of Thomas Robert Malthus*, vols 5 and 6, London, W. Pickering, 1986.

Mantoux, P., *The Industrial Revolution in the Eighteenth Century*, rev. edn, New York, Harper Torchbooks, 1961; orig. pub. 1928.

Mill, J.S., *Principles of Political Economy with Some of their Applications to Social Philosophy* (ed. J.M. Robson), 2 vols, Toronto, Macmillan of Canada, 1966.

Miller, E., *The Abbey and Bishopric of Ely: The Social History of an Eccelesiastical Estate from the Tenth Century to the Early Fourteenth Century*, Cambridge, Cambridge University Press, 1951.

Miller, E. and Hatcher, J., *Medieval England: Rural Society and Economic Change, 1086–1348*, London & New York, Longman, 1978.

Mitchell, B.R., *British Historical Statistics*, Cambridge, Cambridge University Press, 1988.

Mitchell, B.R. and Deane, P., *Abstract of British Historical Statistics*, Cambridge, Cambridge University Press, 1962.

Mokyr, J., *The Lever of Riches: Technological Creativity and Economic Progress*, New York, Oxford University Press, 1990.

Mokyr, J. (ed.), *The British Industrial Revolution: An Economic Perspective*, Boulder, San Francisco and Oxford, Westview Press, 1993.

Mokyr, J., 'Editor's introduction: the new economic history and the industrial revolution', in J. Mokyr (ed.), *The British Industrial Revolution: An Economic Perspective*, Boulder, San Francisco and Oxford, Westview Press, 1993, pp. 1–131.

Mokyr, J. and O'Grada, C., 'Emigration and poverty in pre-famine Ireland', *Explorations in Economic History*, 19, 1982, pp. 360–84.

Nef, J.U., *The Rise of the British Coal Industry*, 2 vols, London, Routledge, 1932; repr. New York, 1972.

Nef, J.U., 'The progress of technology and the growth of large-scale industry in Britain, 1540–1640', *Economic History Review*, 5, 1934, pp. 3–24.

Nicholas, S. and Oxley, D., 'The living standards of women during the industrial revolution, 1795–1820', *Economic History Review*, 2nd ser., 46, November 1993, pp. 723–49.

Nicholas, S. and Shergold, P., 'Intercounty labour mobility during the industrial revolution: evidence from Australian Transportation Records', *Oxford Economic Papers*, 39, 1987, pp. 624–40.

Nicholas, S. and Shergold, P., 'Internal migration in England, 1818–1839', *Journal of Historical Geography*, 13, 1987, pp. 155–68.

Nicholas, S. and Steckel, R., 'Heights and living standards of English workers during the early years of industrialisation, 1770–1815', *Journal of Economic History*, 51, 1991, pp. 937–57.

North, D. and Thomas, R.P., 'The rise and fall of the manorial system: a theoretical model', *Journal of Economic History*, 31, 1971, pp. 777–803.

North, D. and Thomas, R.P., *The Rise of the Western World*, Cambridge, Cambridge University Press, 1973.

O'Brien, P.K., 'Agriculture and the home market for English industry, 1660–1820', *English History Review*, 100, 1985, pp. 773–99.

Oliphant, M., 'The condition of women', *Blackwood's Edinburgh Magazine*, 83, 1858.

Oxley, D., 'Women transported: gendered images and realities', *Australian and New Zealand Journal of Criminology*, 24, 1991, pp. 83–98.

Pahl, R.E., *Divisions of Labour*, Oxford, Blackwell, 1984.

Parkes, B.R., *Essays on Women's Work*, 2nd edn, London, A. Strahan, 1865.

Persson, K.G., *Pre-Industrial Economic Growth*, Oxford, Blackwell, 1988.

Persson, K.G., 'Labour productivity in medieval agriculture: Tuscany and the "low countries"', in B.M.S. Campbell and M. Overton (eds), *Land, Labour and Livestock: Historical Studies in European Agricultural Productivity*, Manchester & New York, Manchester University Press, 1991, pp. 124–43.

Philips, D., *Crime and Authority in Victorian England: The Black Country 1835–1860*, London, Croom Helm, 1977.

Phillips, J.R.S., *The Medieval Expansion of Europe*, Oxford, Clarendon Press, 1988.

Pinchbeck, I., *Women Workers and the Industrial Revolution, 1750–1850*, London, G. Routledge, 1930.

Pinchbeck, I. and Hewitt, M., *Children in English Society*, 2 vols, London, Routledge & Kegan Paul, 1969, 1973.

Pitt, M.M., Rosenzweig, M.R. and Hassan, Md.N., 'Productivity, health and inequality in the intrahousehold distribution of food in low-income countries', *Australian Economic Review*, 80, 1990, pp. 1139–56.

Platt, C., *Medieval England: A Social History and Archaeology from the Conquest to A.D.1600*, London, Routledge and Kegan Paul, 1978.

Pollard, S., 'A new estimate of British coal production, 1750–1850', *Economic History Review*, 2nd ser., 33, 1980, pp. 212–35.

Poos, L.R., *A Rural Society after the Black Death: Essex, 1350–1525*, Cambridge, Cambridge University Press, 1991.

Postan, M.M., *The Medieval Economy and Society: An Economic History of Britain in the Middle Ages*, Harmondsworth, Penguin, 1972.

Quale, G.R., *Families in Context: A World History of Population*, New York, Greenwood Press, 1992.

Rackham, O., *Ancient Woodland: Its History, Vegetation and Uses in England*, London, Edward Arnold, 1980.

Ricardo, D., *On the Principles of Political Economy and Taxation*, in P. Sraffa (ed.), *The Works and Correspondence of David Ricardo*, with the collaboration of M.H. Dobb, Vol. I, Cambridge, Cambridge University Press, 1951.

Richards, E., 'Women in the British economy since about 1700: an interpretation', *History*, 59, 1974, pp. 337–57.

Riden, P., 'The output of the British iron industry before 1870', *Economic History Review*, 2nd ser., 30, 1977, pp. 442–59.

Roberts, M., 'Sickles and scythes: women's work and men's work at harvest time', *History Workshop*, 7, 1979, pp. 3–28.

Rogers, J.E.T., *A History of Agriculture and Prices in England: From the Year after the Oxford Parliament (1259) to the Commencement of the Continental War (1793), Compiled Entirely from Original and Contemporaneous Records*, 7 vols, Oxford, Clarendon Press, 1866–1902.

Romer, P.M., 'Increasing returns and long-run growth', *Journal of Political Economy*, 94, 1986, pp. 1002–37.

Rostow, W.W., *The Stages of Economic Growth: A Non-Communist Manifesto*, Cambridge, Cambridge University Press, 1960.

Rudé, G., *Criminal and Victim: Crime and Society in Early Nineteenth Century England*, Oxford, Oxford University Press, 1985.

Schofield, R.S., 'The geographical distribution of wealth in England, 1334–1649', *Economic History Review*, 2nd ser., 18, December 1965, pp. 483–510.

Schofield, R.S., 'Age-specific mobility in an eighteenth century rural English parish', *Annales de démographie historique*, 1970, pp. 260–74.

Schofield, R.S., 'Dimensions of illiteracy, 1750–1850', *Explorations in Economic History*, 10, 1973, pp. 437–54.

Scott, J.W., *Gender and Politics in History*, New York, Columbia University Press, 1988.

Scrimshaw, N., 'Interactions of malnutrition and infection: advances in understanding', in R.E. Olson (ed.), *Protein-Calorie Malnutrition*, New York, Academic Press, 1975, pp. 353–67.

Seccombe, W., 'Patriarchy stabilized: the construction of the male breadwinner wage norm in nineteenth-century Britain', *Social History*, 2, 1986, pp. 53–76.

Sen, A., 'More than 100 million women are missing', *New York Review of Books*, 37, 1990, pp. 61–6.

Sen, A. and Sengupta, S., 'Malnutrition of rural children and the sex bias', *Economic and Political Weekly*, 18, 1983, pp. 855–64.

Shammas, C., 'The eighteenth-century English diet and economic change', *Explorations in Economic History*, 21, 1984, pp. 254–69.

Shorter, E., *The Making of the Modern Family*, New York, Basic Books, 1975.

Shorter, E., 'Women's work: what difference did capitalism make?', *Theory and Society*, 3, 1976, pp. 513–27.

Shorter, E., *A History of Women's Bodies*, New York, Basic Books, 1982.

Smith, A., *An Inquiry into the Nature and Causes of the Wealth of Nations* (ed. E. Cannan), 2 vols, London, Methuen, 1904; Chicago, 1976.

Smith, R.M., 'Demographic developments in rural England, 1300–1348: a survey', in B.M.S. Campbell (ed.), *Before the Black Death: Studies in the 'Crisis' of the Early Fourteenth Century*, Manchester & New York, Manchester University Press, 1991, pp. 25–77.

Smith Baker, R., 'The social results of the employment of girls and women in factories and workshops', *Transactions of the National Association for the Promotion of Social Science*, 12, 1868.

Snell, K.D.M., 'Agricultural seasonal employment, the standard of living and women's work in the south and east, 1690–1810', *Economic History Review*, 2nd ser., 34, 1981, pp.417–37.

Snell, K.D.M., *Annals of the Labouring Poor: Social Change and Agrarian England, 1660–1900*, Cambridge, Cambridge University Press, 1985.

Snooks, G.D., 'Estimating Australian household labour services, 1881–1986', *Working Papers in Economic History*, No. 130, Australian National University, December 1989.

Snooks, G.D., 'Economic growth during the last millennium: a quantitative perspective for the British Industrial Revolution', *Working Papers in Economic History*, No. 140, Australian National University, July 1990.

Snooks, G.D., 'Arbitrary decree or rational calculation? The contribution of Domesday Book to economic history and economics', *Australian Economic History Review*, 30, September 1990, pp. 23–49.

Snooks, G.D., *Economics without Time: A Science Blind to the Forces of Historical Change*, London, Macmillan, 1993.

Snooks, G.D., *Portrait of the Family within the Total Economy: A Study in Longrun Dynamics: Australia, 1788–1990*, Cambridge, Cambridge University Press, 1994.

Snooks, G.D., 'The dynamic role of the market in the Anglo-Norman economy and beyond, 1086–1300', in R. Britnell and B. Campbell (eds), *A Commercialising Economy: England 1086–1300*, Manchester, Manchester University Press, forthcoming 1994.

Snooks, G.D. and McDonald, J., *Domesday Economy: A New Approach to Anglo-Norman History*, Oxford, Clarendon Press, 1986.

Stanton, T. (ed.), *The Woman Question in Europe: A Series of Original Essays*, London, S. Low, Marston, Searle, and Rivington, 1884.

Steckel, R.H., 'Height and per capita income', *Historical Methods*, 16, 1986, pp. 1–7.

Steckel, R.H., 'Stature and living standards in the United States', in R. Gallman and J. Wallis (eds), *The Standard of Living in Early Nineteenth Century America*, Chicago (forthcoming).

Stone, R., 'Some seventeenth century econometrics: consumers' behaviour', *Revue Européenne des Sciences Sociales*, 26, 1988, pp. 19–41.

Stone, R., 'When will the war end?', *Cambridge Journal of Economics*, 12, 1988, pp. 193–201.

Stone, R., 'Some seventeenth century econometrics: public finance', *Revue Européenne des Sciences Sociales*, 26, 1989, pp. 5–32.

Tanner, J.M., *Growth of Adolescence*, Oxford, Blackwell Scientific Publications, [1955]1962.

Thomas, J., 'Women and capitalism: oppression or emancipation? A review article', *Comparative Studies in Social History*, 30, 1988, pp. 534–49.

Thompson, E.P., *The Making of the English Working Class*, London, V.Gollancz, 1963.

Tilly, L.A. and Scott, J.W., *Women, Work and Family*, New York, Holt, Rinehart and Winston, 1978.

Titow, J.Z., *English Rural Society, 1200–1350*, London, Allen & Unwin, 1969.

Toynbee, A., *Toynbee's Industrial Revolution: A Reprint of Lectures on the Industrial Revolution*, New York and Newton Abbot, David and Charles, 1969; orig. pub. 1884.

United Kingdom, Commissioners for Inquiring into the Condition of the Unemployed Hand-Loom Weavers in the United Kingdom, 'Hand-Loom Weavers: Report of the Commissioners, with Appendix [19 February 1841]' (*P.P.*, Session 1841, No. 296, Vol. X), in *Irish University*

Press Series of British Parliamentary Papers – Industrial Revolution: Textiles, 10, Shannon; Irish University Press, 1970.

United Kingdom, Commissioners on the Employment of Children, Young Persons, and Women in Agriculture, 'First Report of the Commissioners on the employment of children, young persons, and women in agriculture', *Parliamentary Papers*, Session 1867–68, No. 4068, Vol. XVII.

United Kingdom, Parliament, 'Report from the Select Committee on Education of the Poorer Classes in England and Wales, together with Minutes of Evidence and Index [13 July 1838]' (*P.P.*, 2nd Session 1837–38, No. 589, Vol. VII), in *Irish University Press Series of British Parliamentary Papers – Education: Poorer Classes, 6*, Shannon; Irish University Press, 1970, pp. 513–699.

United Kingdom, Parliament, '1841 Census Great Britain: Statements on population; enumeration abstract; indexes to place names' (*P.P.*, 2nd Session 1841, No. 52, Vol. II), in *Irish University Press Series of British Parliamentary Papers – Population, 3*, Shannon; Irish University Press, 1971.

United Kingdom, Parliament, 'Report of the Commissioners appointed to take the Census of Ireland for the Year 1841, with Appendix and Index' (*P.P.*, Session 1843, No. 504, Vol. XXIV), in *Irish University Press Series of British Parliamentary Papers – Population, 2*, Shannon; Irish University Press, 1968.

White, L.P. and Plaskett, L.G., *Biomass as Fuel*, London & New York, Academic Press, 1981.

Williamson, J.G., 'The structure of pay in Britain, 1710–1911', *Research in Economic History*, 7, 1982, pp. 1–54.

Williamson, J.G., *Did British Capitalism Breed Inequality?* London, Allen & Unwin, 1985.

Wright, J.S., 'On the employment of women in factories in Birmingham', *Transactions of the National Association for the Promotion of Social Science*, 1, 1857.

Wrigley, E.A., 'The growth of population in eighteenth-century England: a conundrum resolved', *Past and Present*, 98, 1983, pp. 121–50.

Wrigley, E.A., 'Urban growth and agricultural change: England and the continent in the early modern period', *Journal of Interdisciplinary History*, XV, 1985, pp. 683–728.

Wrigley, E.A., *Continuity, Chance and Change: The Character of the Industrial Revolution in England*, Cambridge, Cambridge University Press, 1988.

Wrigley, E.A., 'Malthus on the prospects for the labouring poor', *Historical Journal*, 31, 1988, pp. 813–29.

Wrigley, E.A., 'Two kinds of capitalism, two kinds of growth', *LSE Quarterly*, 2, 1988, pp. 97–121.

Wrigley, E.A. and Schofield, R.S., *The Population History of England, 1541–1871: A Reconstruction*, London, Edward Arnold, 1981.

Young, A.A., *Economic Problems, New and Old*, Boston, Houghton Mifflin, 1927.

Young, M.D. and Willmott, P., *The Symmetrical Family: A Study of Work and Leisure in the London Region*, London, Routledge & Kegan Paul, 1973.

INDEX

(All references are to England unless otherwise indicated)